T0171601

SON OF A DRESS MAKER

Life and Struggle of a Foreign Medical Graduate in USA

by

Dr. Carlos Cruz Soriano, M.D. FACAS (retired)

authorHOUSE®

AuthorHouse™
1663 Liberty Drive
Bloomington, IN 47403
www.authorhouse.com
Phone: 1-800-839-8640

First published by AuthorHouse 2/11/2011

ISBN: 978-1-4567-1931-9 (sc)
ISBN: 978-1-4567-1932-6 (e)
ISBN: 978-1-4567-1933-3 (dj)

Library of Congress Control Number: 2010918949

Printed in the United States of America

Table of Contents

Dedication

To my grandmother, Urbana Cruz; my dearest mother, Inicita Cruz; my uncle, Felipe Cruz; and attorney Manolo Cruz, may your souls rest in peace, and to my aunt, Lupe, whom I spent part of my formative years with: My character and the person I am now are due to all of you and the nurturing and guidance you gave me, your will and determination for me to succeed in life, your endurance, and your undying love for me. These attributes contributed to my relentless pursuit of higher education and instilled the wisdom I needed to achieve my goals. Lastly, to my father despite his shortcomings and got lost in the chaos of human nature.

To my sister Luzviminda S. Cabuay (deceased) and my younger sister Baby Inicita S. Maslog, thank you for your love.

To my dearest wife, who helped me relentlessly during my difficult years in college and who cared for and loved my children during my absence while I was in training, my wholehearted appreciation!

To my children, Christine, Cheryl (deceased), Charles, and Chad, who grew up and were nurtured by their mother, please forgive me for not having the time that I wanted to spend with you. My goal was to provide you with financial security for your college education. I never had those luxuries when I was growing up and during my college years. I have tried my best for us to be together on our several long extended vacations; these, at least, I managed very well.

To my six lovely grandchildren, Libby, Bootchie, Ally, Zoe, Maddy, and R.J. Soriano, without a doubt you will succeed in your lives when I am gone. I can see in you the brilliance of your minds.

I dedicate this book to all of you.

CHAPTER 1

Flashback: The Spanish-American War and World War II

I was born November 3, 1939, in a small town of San Miguel in the province of Bulacan about seventy miles north of Manila. In my family, I was the first-born male in my generation; all of my first cousins were females. It took fourteen years before another male cousin was born.

A few miles from San Miguel is another small town called Biyak-na-Bato, which means cracked or split stone. The town has a cave where General Emilio Aguinaldo, who later became the first president of the Philippines, retreated from Spanish troops during the revolution against Spain. The rebels were called Katipuneros. On July 7, 1897, shortly after his arrival, he assembled the leaders of the revolution to draft the new constitution for the Filipino nation. On November 1, 1897, the drafted constitution was approved. It was known as the Biyak-na-Bato Constitution. It was basically a copy of the

1

constitution written in 1895 by the Cubans, who were also in revolt against Spanish rule.

Shortly after the approval of the constitution, the Biyak-na-Bato Republic was proclaimed, and General Emilio Aguinaldo was elected president. The Spanish governor of the Philippines, realizing that he could not crush the revolution made a deal with the rebels. On December 15, 1897, the Pact of Biyak-na-Bato was signed by both parties, and General Aguinaldo was exiled to Hong Kong as part of the agreement. Both sides violated the pact, and no real peace was achieved. The amnesty that had been pledged by Spain was not granted. The Spanish authorities arrested and imprisoned the patriots who had surrendered their arms.

Outbreak of the Spanish-American War

The island of Cuba, like the Philippines, also suffered under Spanish rule. Like Filipinos, they rose in revolt against Spain many times. On February 15, 1898, the U.S. battleship *Maine* was blown up in Havana Harbor, causing the death of many Americans. The cause of the explosion was unknown; the present-day theory was that the coal ignited inside the ship, setting off a chain reaction in which the gunpowder inside the ship was ignited. Whatever the cause, the American public became furious and aroused the nation's war spirit, hence the slogan and battle cry "Remember the *Maine*!". In April 1898 the U.S. Congress passed a resolution for Spain to leave Cuba. Spain declared war on the United States on April 14, ushering in the Spanish-American War.

Commodore George Dewey, commanding the American Asiatic Squadron, was in Hong Kong and received orders from the War Department to proceed to the Philippines and destroy the Spanish fleet, which he did with ease because he had an iron armada of battleships. The Filipinos helped the Americans take control of the Philippines from the Spaniards. General Aguinaldo established a dictatorship on May 4, 1898, followed by the proclamation of the Philippine Independence on June 12, 1898.

Commissioners from the United States and Spain met in Paris to make a peace treaty. On December 10, 1898, the treaty was signed: Spain would cede the Philippines, Guam, and Puerto Rico to the United States, and they will leave Cuba. The United States would pay Spain twenty million dollars.

The following year, on January 23, 1899, the First Philippine Republic was inaugurated in Malolos Bulacan; it was never recognized by the United States and foreign powers, but it was supported by majority of Filipinos.

Dr. Carlos Cruz Soriano, M.D. FACAS (retired)

Filipino-American Conflict
(1899–1902)

The first blow of the Filipino-American conflict was struck by America when a Nebraska volunteer shot and killed a Filipino soldier who was crossing the American lines on the San Juan Bridge. Hostilities started on both sides, and General Arthur MacArthur proceeded to Malolos to capture General Aguinaldo. Fleeing from the advancing Americans, Aguinaldo moved from town to town but was eventually captured. He was brought back to Manila at Malacanang Palace and, to his surprise, was graciously received by General Arthur MacArthur. The Americans went south, which was still occupied by some Spaniards, but it eventually fell into American hands. In the southern part of the Philippines are the islands of Mindanao and Jolo, where the Filipino Muslim live; the inhabitants were called Moros. The Americans had a hard time stopping the rebellion. The Moros has the habit of running amok, charged up and ready to die. They charged toward the Americans; their sidearms were just six-shooter .38-caliber revolvers. That did not stop the Moros from hacking the Americans with *bolos* (machetes) despite their six rounds of shots. In 1911, Colt .45-caliber semi-automatic sidearms came into play; they had stopping power, which was the reason they were invented: to stop the charging Moros. It remained the American army's sidearm in World War II.

Democratization of the Philippines

The greatest legacy of America to the Filipino people is democracy, just as Christianity is Spain's legacy. Filipinos also acquired an inferiority complex during the Spanish regime because the Spaniards look down on the Filipinos as an inferior race; this changed when the Americans came. We came to believe that we had an inherent right to life, liberty, and the pursuit of happiness and that all men are equal before the law, irrespective of race, color, creed, or social position.

The United States never intended to hold the Philippines as a colony forever and intended to grant the Philippines independence as soon as the people were capable of governing themselves. Military commanders governed the Philippines for the president of the United States. Several Philippine commissions were established to determine whether the people were ready to govern themselves. The civil government was slowly being formed and organized during these years; in 1907 the first Philippine Assembly was formed.

The country made great strides in economics and social progress. The Bureau of Lands was established to safeguard the land for the people, and the Bureau of Agriculture to promote agriculture. Roads and bridges were developed, and the modern telephone, radio, and wireless telegraphy were introduced. The mail service was improved.

An outstanding achievement of America in the Philippines

was the improvement of public health. The epidemics of cholera, small pox, and bubonic plaque were eliminated.

The Filipino people, in appreciation of American policy and as a gesture of loyalty, stopped their pursuit of independence and joined the American government in its war efforts when the United States entered the First World War (1914–1918). The Philippine legislature offered twenty-five thousand troops to fight in Europe. About six thousand Filipinos joined the Navy, and four thousand from Hawaii joined the army.

Another major American contribution was to education. For the first time in Philippine history, education was no longer the privilege of a few rich families. It had become the right of all people, rich and poor, to be educated. It was clear that democracy would only survive if the people were educated.

The governments that America established in the Philippines from the military government (1898–1901) to the Commonwealth of the Philippines (1935–1946) were in accordance with its democratic principle.

America also introduced into the country two basic concepts of democracy: popular election and the separation of church and state.

On November 15, 1935, the Commonwealth of the Philippines was inaugurated in Luneta, Manila. Present at this historic event were guests from the United States: the vice president, the secretary of war, the president of the Senate, the speaker of the House of Representatives, General Douglas MacArthur, and Governor General Francis Burton. The newly elected president of the Philippines, Manual Quezon, and Vice President Osmena.

On July 26, 1941, General Douglas MacArthur, military adviser to the Philippine Commonwealth, was called back to active service. He was appointed by President Roosevelt as commander of the newly organized United States Armed Forces in the Far East. One hundred thousand Filipinos were inducted as soldiers under his command.

On December 7, 1941, the Japanese made a sneak air attack on Pearl Harbor almost destroying the U.S. Naval Fleet. A few hours later the Japanese air squadron attacked Davao, a city in Mindanao, followed by an attack on Luzon—mainly Clark Field, where the American Air Force was completely destroyed on the ground. On December 10, the Japanese invasion of the Philippines started. The Japanese landed on various parts of the islands. General MacArthur could not stop the enemy landings because of lack of air and naval support. By December 31, 1941, General MacArthur had completed the retreat of his northern and southern armies to Bataan, where he made his last stand against the enemy. On January 1942 the battle of Bataan began. The Filipino-American troops faced a hopeless situation. They had no air or naval support and were faced with shortages of food, medicine, and ammunitions. The president of the Commonwealth and War

Cabinets secretly left Corregidor by submarine and eventually reached San Francisco by boat. Gen MacArthur left with his family by PT boats, safely reached Mindanao, and then took a plane to Australia. On May 6, 1942, Corregidor fell after five months of fighting, which saved Australia from being invaded by the Japanese.

In the infamous "Death March" that followed the Japanese invasion and the fall of Corregidor, American and Filipino soldiers died side by side. Many escaped and were assisted by Filipino civilians, eventually forming the Philippine resistance against the Japanese Imperial Army.

During the Japanese occupation of the Philippines, food was very hard to come by. Luckily we lived in the province, and my grandmother planted vegetables and fruits for us to consume. My mother told me that I was fed peanuts and *salabat* (similar to ginger ale), which was made with boiling water, ginger, and brown sugar. The peanuts had a lot of protein and an oleic acid, a monosaturated omega-9 fatty acid commonly found in olive oil, soybeans, corn, and sunflower seeds. These are all necessary ingredients for the metabolism of brain function.

I have a few memories of the time before Gen. Douglas MacArthur returned to the Philippines in late 1944. I was about five years old then. I can remember the "dog fights" up in the air between the Americans and the Japanese Zeros and the bombings nearby. I can vividly remember during the bombings that we had to evacuate from one place to another in our province to escape the onslaught. In one instance, a bomb blasted nearby, and the loudness shook me up; I was stunned by it. My uncle, Felipe, slapped my face to wake me up, and I started crying. We moved from one house to the other; in the house that I remember we stayed on the ground level because it was a little crowded upstairs on the main floor.

The typical houses in the barrios were made with tree trunks as the main frame of the house, connected by bamboo trusses and covered by webs of palm leaves covering the walls. The roofs were made of stalks of palm leaves, laid one on top of the other. The floors were made of strips of bamboo with the shiny parts exposed as the floors of the house. Our basic sleeping paraphernalia were mosquito nets, webs of palm leaves for our sleeping mats, pillows filled with chicken feathers, and urinals. The rationale for having the urinal (called an *arinola*) was that it could be used at night instead of going outside the house to the outhouse. Well, one particular night, the owner of the house somehow managed to tip over the urinal, spilling the contents all over us down below. We politely informed the owner of the house about the accident, and because of the embarrassing situation, he allowed us to sleep with them on the second floor.

These traumatic incidents have stayed with me since that time. War is very traumatic to the most vulnerable—children.

You think children will easily forget such things? No way! That is why I protected my children from sources of inside and outside trauma. I was careful of what I said to them because I knew that they would remember my words. My wife was very good at nurturing and raising them the right way. My children's dispositions and their determination were very good. They were good in school and also excellent at raising their own children, especially Christine, who raised her two daughters, Ally and Zoe, on her own without the help of my wife. These two girls are just amazing; they could read and write before going to first grade.

CHAPTER 2

Post-War Period

Balik-Balik

After the war, during the liberation of Manila, we decided to move to Manila. My grandmother's entire house in San Miguel was dismantled and rebuilt on Main Street in Sampaloc. During the process of rebuilding we rented a house in Balik-Balik, a suburb of Manila just a few miles from Sampaloc, which is part of metro Manila.

My sister Luzviminda was born at this time. I can remember that Manila was littered with small shacks selling war surplus items. Spam, the canned meat brought by the GIs, became our staple food for quite a long time. It was an uneventful period of my life until I got exposed to pornography. I was assigned to run the 16mm projector manually to show pornographic films brought by the GIs from the States, usually black-and-white silent films made during the 1920s or '30s. I didn't even know what I was watching; it just looked like a man and a woman fooling around with each other. How would I know? I was just a six-year-old boy!

A whorehouse was just next door to us too. I can remember a lot of white rubbers laying around outside the whorehouse. The children picked them up and blew air into them, inflating them like balloons. I was told not to play with them. I found out later that they were condoms used by the GIs and thrown out of the windows after their sexcapades. I didn't even know what condoms were until somebody told me what they were for. I still don't understand!

Before dismantling the house in San Miguel, from time to time we would go back to visit my grandmother for a few days, riding horses and water buffalos. Her house was just outside the town, and we had to used a horse-drawn carriage called a *kalesa* to get to her place. It was fun to get out of the city and be in a country, and I enjoyed the peacefulness and scenery. My grandmother showed me how to cook, feed the chickens and pigs, and do all the other domestic stuff that should be done.

Sampaloc, Main Street

We did not stay too long in Balik-Balik after my grandmother's house was relocated and rebuilt in the Sampaloc district. The location was great; it was in the middle of a business area, with a nearby market, movie theaters, and schools. The neighborhood was crowded with shanty homes and good homes as well. I do believe that this was where I started my formative years.

My mother opened a dress shop on the first floor of the house, and we slept in the back of the house. The house has three and a half bedrooms, and one bedroom was being rented to a college student studying law at the University of Manila Law School nearby. My mother's business picked up a little bit, and she started to hire some help. She hired a specialized dressmaker called a *bordadora*. These dressmakers used sewing machines to make intricate patterns like flowers or other designs on clothes. Now this is done by computerized machines.

I can still remember her pretty face. She came from Laguna province just south of Manila. She eventually got married to one of the law students who had just finished up his schooling. Most of the law students who came from the southern part of the Philippines were Muslims; and this was where my aunt Lupe met her husband. He was a law student at the University of Manila. In my recollection of events that followed, he got very sick and was in bed for weeks. Aunt Lupe was the one taking care of him. He lost his hair and started developing blisters all over his body. During my college years, when I was studying medicine, I theorized that this was a severe allergic reaction to penicillin. Penicillin had just been invented and was given to the troops to reduce the mortality rate of the war tremendously and also was also given to civilians for whatever sicknesses they had. In those days we didn't know much about allergic reactions or sensitivity to drugs like penicillin; we found out the hard way—anaphylactic shock and sometimes death!

Sampaloc district has many schools nearby, including universities and my high school alma mater San Sebastian College. This district was designated a "school belt" in metro Manila. The official residence of the Republic of the Philippines, Malacanang Palace, was just around the corner, facing the Pasig River.

There was an older woman who lived in our house for a short period of time. Being a kid I didn't pay much attention to her, but she smiled and was nice to me all the time. My sister Luzviminda told me her story many years later when we were in New York. I was a surgical resident in Jamaica Hospital then, and Luzviminda had just migrated to the United States with her husband Jun Cabuay. We had a little chat during dinner, and she said, "Carling [my nickname], do you remember that old woman in Sampaloc when we were young?"

I said "Yes, I do."

"She is the mother of our dad!"

I was silent for about a second and then I said, "What is going on?"

My sister began explaining that our dad was born out of wedlock to this woman who had been a maid in the household of my grandfather (whom I never met). My dad and I never communicated, and he never told me anything about his family or where he came from. The only thing I remember about him was that he beat me up when I was a kid, to the point that I wanted to fight back. I told my grandmother about it and said that I wanted to leave home to stay away from him. My grandmother never said anything bad about my dad, though; she just lectured me to finish school and leave. And that was what I did.

My grandmother also told me that my father left my mother for two years with me as an infant during the Japanese occupation. When he got back, he told my grandmother that he was wanted by the Japanese. I could never understand my father's behavior when I was a kid. When he got upset or mad, he would hit the floor and start jerking all his extremities. My sister also revealed to me that our dad was raised by two of his father's sisters, left for Spain before the Japanese came. On one instance, he stood outside our house with a machete and started cursing and shouting at my grandmother and my mother who were inside the house. After the incident, my grandmother left and built a few rental houses with the help of my uncle Manolo just outside metro Manila in Balintawak, an area near the university for agriculture (the Araneta Institute of Agriculture).

I finally understood my father's behavior when I was in the college of medicine learning about psychology, which is the study of human mind. The jerking of his extremities was just a show to attract attention, which he probably never had when he was growing up. He transferred that anger at his father to me; maybe that was his reason for beating me up so badly at times that even today I can't forgot the trauma of it. I cannot blame him for keeping silent about his past, and I cannot say much about him because I don't know him well enough. This is just my hypothesis of his problem; he got lost somewhere in his life in the chaos of human nature.

We stayed on Main Street in Sampaloc for about two years. They were fun years for me, and I tried to learn as much as I could. I learned how to use the sewing machine and make toys with my bare hands to sell to my friends; and I also learned how to gamble at an early age, sometimes winning dimes. In my spare time I tried to read comic books and saw movies by myself at the theater that was walking distance from our house. For twenty-five cents I could view double-feature films, the original Batman, Captain Marvel, Captain America, and Rocket Man—and of course Johnny Weissmuller's Tarzan movies. Learning how to use the sewing machine, I made a Batman costume from an old green GI blanket, crafting the hood with bat ears and cape in one piece.

On one particular afternoon before the sun set, I was outside the house reading comic books when I saw that the top floor of our house was on fire. My parents were out at the time, and when the firefighters came there was chaos in the streets. The small shack where I was reading the comic books caught fire because of the intense heat. My neighbors helped me take some of the sewing machines and furniture out of the house. The rest was burned to ashes. It was a very traumatic experience for me emotionally and physically. Losing a house and just about all one's belongings is just too much for anybody to take.

My parents decided to look for an area nearby to open a new dress shop because all our customers where located in and around the area. It was just good business sense not to leave the area. Luzviminda and I were still kids, so of course we went along with whatever decision our parents made.

On July 17, 1949 my second sister was born at Mary Chiles Hospital, a block or two away from our house on Main Street. She was named Inicita, after my mother. She now lives in Jacksonville, Florida.

CHAPTER 3

La Inicita's Dress Shop

After the fire, we moved to Legarda Street, a main thoroughfare for the passenger jeepneys, surplus vehicles left over from the war and converted into commercial passenger vehicles that had different routes going to different destinations within metro Manila complex. Depending on your destination, you just had to know where to stop and pick up another one.

We lived in this dress shop from when we were in primary school and up through college. It was our custom that all the children in the family should go to school. We learned this from the Americans during their stint to democratize the Philippines. English was being taught in the schools from primary school and up through college. That made the Philippines the third largest English-speaking nation in the world behind the United Kingdom. Because of our ability to speak English, Filipinos were the greatest exports to the world, from every corner of the earth, cruise ships, commercial shipping and so much more.

Santa Rita Elementary School

The shop was thriving steadily during my formative years. My parents were able to send us to private schools nearby. I learned how to cook, wash clothes with my bare hands, and iron with the old charcoal-heated iron. Being a boy I was the domestic help. Whenever we had a family gathering I was assigned to cook. We had frequent visits from our relatives and uncles.

My sister and I went to school in Santa Rita Elementary School, and my father's half brother walked us to school every day. The school was run by sisters; I don't remember which order they belonged to. My school days were stormy at times; I learned how to protect myself against bullies in school. I was caught several times fighting with my classmate; and my teacher got sick and tired of me fighting, so I was punished by being placed in the corner of the room with tape on my mouth. Most of my classmates were *mestizos*, half Spanish and half Filipino. They are good looking, and some them became movie stars.

One morning on my way to school, as I walking on the sidewalk, I saw a young girl get hit by a jeepney. There was blood all over, and she was unconscious. I wanted to help, but what did I know? I was just a kid. The blood did not bother me, though, and the gruesome situation stayed in my mind. I knew then that I wanted to be a doctor someday.

San Sebastian College

My sister and I went separate ways in our secondary and high schooling. She went to La Consolacion College for girls, and I went to San Sebastian College for boys. Both were walking distance from our dress shop.

My mom bought a used piano, and both of us were taught by a piano teacher who was hired on an hourly basis. We were taught for years, and I was pretty good at it. In fact was able to memorize and play Tchaikovsky's Piano Concerto No. 1 by heart. Up to this day I can still remember some of the chords.

In high school I befriended a boy named George Gonzalez; he was pure Spanish and smart. Together we built a radio receiver from scratch, and I built model airplanes from balsa wood and rubber powered All the planes I built were all hanging in our dress shop. I made a blueprint of a miniature Eiffel Tower and constructed it about four feet high with toothpicks glued with Duco Cement. I kept it in the shop for several years.

At San Sebastian College during its infancy, all or most of the school's students had been kicked out of other schools.

They were Spanish boys and some mestizos who were spoiled brats but brilliant students. I got to know them better because I used to hang out with them. After any basketball game or tournament there would be a fistfight among the gangs from the schools.

At my school there was a vacant lot just outside the school compound, and we used this lot for boxing matches almost every day after school. The word would get around about who was going to fight who!

Life went on on Legarda Street. The dress shop was still on the positive side financially. We were able to hire some domestic help, and that was good news—no more domestic duties for me.

At the beginning of every school year, my mother used to say to me, "Carlos, let's go to your school so you can introduce me to your teachers." We went, and she got to know my teachers. I never knew why. I found out later that she talked to them just to make sure they would pass me in my subjects. My grades in school up to the second year of high school were terrible, barely passing with 75 percent on the nose.

One day while I was ironing my clothes, my mom and dad were lying on the floor resting and talking to each other. Poor people talk of big things in life, daydreams just to keep them going, motivate them, and help them to keep their sanity. I was in my second year of high school then, and that particular day woke me up to the fact that I had to do something. Being the firstborn male, I had the responsibility to save my family. If I didn't, there was no telling what would happen in the future.

SAN SEBASTIAN COLLEGE
HIGH SCHOOL 1956

Tackling the Odds

Wasting no time, during my summer vacation after my second year in high school, I enrolled in a vocational school, Underwood Business Institute, to learn typing and Gregg's shorthand. I spent the whole summer learning the trade that I would use for my entire life. When I graduated, I was able to type ninety words a minute. As I write this book I am using my skills as a typist. I am using an electric IBM Wheelwriter 2, not the old Underwood typewriter with which I had to use every muscle in my fingers to punch the keys. My teacher in the vocational school saw me the following school year in San Sebastian College because his son was also enrolled there.

He was shocked when he saw me and asked, "What are you doing here?"

I answered, "Sir, I am in my third year of high school." Usually vocational school was for those students who had graduated from high school.

"Is that so?"

"Yes, sir, I have a lot of catching up to do."

He smiled and left after dropping his son at school. Underwood Business Institute was right across the street from San Sebastian College.

One day I decided to walk to the University of Santo Tomas College of Medicine. I could make the trip in about thirty minutes because I knew the area pretty well and took shortcuts; otherwise it would have taken at least an hour of walking. I went to the registrar of the college, picked up some brochures, and inquired about the entry qualification. I was informed that I should have a grade of at least 85 percent in high school to get admitted to the preparatory course, the equivalent of a pre-med associate of arts degree in the United States. I thought to myself, *How can I raise my grade from 75 percent to 85 percent?* Boy, was I in big trouble!

From my third year to my fourth year in high school, I really worked and studied very hard. I quit fooling around with my friends and hit the books. I never got any grade below 95 percent, including on quizzes and major examinations. In the last few months before my graduation from high school. The principal, Rev. Father Alehandro Ramirez, summoned me to his office. I was a bit nervous before I walked in, wondering what I had done wrong.

I asked him, "Father, what did I do?"

He answered, "You did nothing, Carlos. I just want to tell you that I cannot give you the valedictorian status because of your grades from the first two years."

"Oh … Father, I am not after that. I just want to have a grade of 85 percent so that I can get admitted to the University of Santo Tomas College of Medicine."

When I graduated from high school, my final grade was 88.9 percent. To get to that grade level I had to hit almost 100 percent on most of my subjects in my last two years. I was exempted in most of the subjects, and I can remember helping my teacher to proctor the final examinations.

My grandmother attended my graduation. She knew that I could be admitted to the University of Santo Tomas to become a medical doctor, and she promised that she would help me with the tuition. She gave me a Parker pen as a gift.

I could have tried to get into some other good school like the University of the Philippines; with my high school grade

I could go anywhere. But the University of the Philippines was located in Quezon City, way out of metro Manila, and it would cost me Pl.50 one-way to commute there. There was no way I could afford that.

The University of Santo Tomas is the oldest university in the Far East. It was founded by the Dominican Friars in 1611. The university is twenty-five years older than Harvard University, the oldest university in the United States. The University of Santo Tomas is the largest Catholic university in the world. In 2011, it will be celebrating four hundred years of existence.

During the summer after my high school graduation, I was busy preparing for college. I had been back and forth to UST, trying to figure out the schedule, the subjects, and the necessary documents for admission. I found out that since it was a Catholic university, the male and female students were separated, including in cafeterias and hallways. There was no chance to meet and mingle with the girls.

Life-Threatening Incidents

I can remember two life-threatening incidents. One occurred when I was about twelve years old and the other when I was in New York during my residency training at Jamaica Hospital.

On weekends, while still living in Legarda, my family

would venture out of Manila to see some attractions like the birthplace of our Philippine hero Dr. Jose Rizal in Calamba Laguna. He was an ophthalmologist and a novelist trained abroad and executed in Luneta under the Spanish regime. In the old Catholic church Las Piñas, a few miles south of Manila, there was a bamboo organ, the only one of its kind in the world. It was built in 1818 by a Spanish priest-musician. The Bamboo Organ of Las Piñas is more than a historical relic of the Filipino Spanish past; it is one of the living glories of Philippine musical art.

The hot springs of Los Baños, Laguna, was also one of the favorite attractions of Filipinos. You could get there by train from Manila. It was located in a small town with hotels and eating places. In the shallow part of the spring were rows of cemented cubicles that families could rent to take baths in the warm spring, which was supposed to have some medicinal properties. We rented a tire inner tube to float in the deeper parts of the spring. The water was crystal clear, and you could see the bottom about twelve to fifteen feet below.

During our trip to Los Baños, I was using the tube, which was a little too big for me, and drifted out into the deeper part of the lagoon. I was holding onto the tube with my arms extended; but the tube was somewhat slippery, and I eventually slipped and went down under. Since I didn't know how to swim, I knew I had to use my head to get out of the situation. I did not panic.

I let myself drop all the way down to the bottom, and as soon as I reached the bottom I kicked very hard to reach the surface, aiming for the hole in the inner tube. I reached my target and held on to it with a sigh of relief. Could it have been my instinct for survival that saved me from drowning? Or could it have be that somebody up there was watching over me?

I noticed as I grew up that I had an uncanny ability to get out of trouble or find my way out if I was boxed in in any situation. This ability would come in handy much later when I was living in New York City with my family. For instance, when I was ill in New York much later, I isolated myself in one room of the house and told my wife not to come in the room because we didn't have a diagnosis for my condition and we had no isolation room in the hospital.

CHAPTER 4

University of Santo Tomas College
of Medicine & Surgery

In June of 1956, I went to the university and enrolled in the preparatory two-year pre-med course. The other students and I, high school graduates from all over the Philippines, not just Manila, were gathered in a big room. We also had some foreign students from China and the United States.

The University of Santo Tomas had been known to filter students and only admit the cream of the crop. They took our report cards and started the screening process. Anybody with an average of 85 percent and above was admitted; the rest were sent home. My friend, whose father was a doctor and owned a small maternity hospital in Sampaloc, was eliminated. We talked and arrived at the conclusion that he should let his father handle the situation. His father called the dean of the College of Medicine. I liked the guy; he was a good friend and came from a well-to-do family. The following day he told me that he had been admitted. I was happy for him and that he would be my classmate.

My friends in Legarda who worked in the barbershop and the tailoring shop as well as my good friend who owned a school supply store were happy for me. We had all grown up together during our formative years. They were all my true friends, unlike the friends one makes after one's formative years, who are just acquaintances. During the first day of the elimination period, the teacher was calling our names to return our report cards. The teacher called my name, and I went to the front of the room. To my astonishment my grades were in the nineties, and the report card is from a different school than the one I had attended. I immediately returned the card to the teacher. Apparently, another student and I had the same name and the same middle initial, C. His stood for Carlos, and mine, for Cruz. The teacher immediately corrected the mistake and gave me my report card. In the pre-med program, we were allowed to use street clothes. There was no uniform. Two years went by, and I had no difficulty with any of the subjects. I realized then that the school I had come from, San Sebastian College, was a good school. During my years in practice in St. Petersburg, Florida, a Filipino told me that San Sebastian College was one of the "Ivy League" schools in Manila, most famous for their school of law.

After our two years of pre-med came another elimination period. After reviewing each student's performance during the two-year period, the school would publish the results and post them on the bulletin board. This was the most nerve-racking period of my life. The names of the students who would be admitted to the college of medicine. Imagine the embarrassment and anxiety a student would feel if his or her name was not listed on the bulletin board! The students who were not admitted went to different schools to pursue their studies for the medical profession. There were quite a few of them in Manila, and getting enrolled was no problem.

After I got the good news, I told my mother and grandmother that I had been admitted in the college of medicine. As I explained, my situation at home, as domestic help, had changed. My mother had hired someone to provide domestic help, including taking care of my uniforms. My uniform was like a Guayabera shirt with two pockets at the bottom of the shirt in front and a small one on the left side of the chest in pure white. You could easily recognize that I was a medical student.

During the rainy season around July and August, Manila streets would flood. Most of the time we didn't have school, but sometimes it could not be avoided. While in school there were occasional downpours of several inches of rain. When I was ready to go home I would take my shoes off and start walking home barefoot. Once in a while I got a ride from my friend who drove a VW Beetle.

Anatomy was the first subject early in the morning at

eight o'clock. I was late most of the time because I slept late at night studying. My anatomy teacher quit calling my name during the roll call because she knew that I would be there late. My quizzes and exams in anatomy were excellent, and I was exempted from taking the finals. I had the gift of visual memory, and anatomy is the hardest subject in medicine. It involves 90 percent memorization of the anatomical structures; the names, origins, insertion points of the muscles, and the organs in the body stayed in my long-term memory. The brain has an inexhaustible capacity to retain huge amounts of data. As I write this book, my short-term memory lasts for about a few seconds but the information can be stored in my long-term memory through continuous repetition in my mind. My typing is sometimes even not fast enough for what comes out of my brain.

Occasionally, while I was studying, my friends in Legarda invited me to go for a drink of San Miguel beer. My window on the second floor of the dress shop was in front of a busy street and all the noise that went with it. My friends would tap my window by throwing small stones, and I would wave my hand in response to let them know that I would be down. They were barbers and making money, so they didn't mind paying for the drinks. And they understood when I said no because I had an exam the following day.

On one occasion, my mother left with my sister to go to visit a relative in San Miguel for the weekend. The next night, a fire started in the wall bordering another shop that did chrome plating. I could not bear the popping sound and went to investigate. I immediately recognized the source of the fire, and when the firefighters came, I told them which wall to break; that stopped the fire from entering our shop, but it went to the roofs and almost destroyed the two businesses on either side of our shop. My neighbor friend helped me by catching the medical books that I threw out the window despite the popping electrical sound and the heat of the fire above my head.

We were able to save the sewing machines and placed them on the opposite side of the road. What bothered me, though, was that a firefighter stole my stethoscope. The fire did not bother me, probably because of when our house had caught fire several years before on Main Street. We fixed the shop, which had mostly suffered water damage, and opened the shop a week later.

During summer vacation, after my second year in medical school, I noticed a girl minding the store in front of our shop. I asked around my neighborhood and found out that her sister owned the shop. I called her to introduce myself, and we became phone pals. I started singing to her on the phone—of course, the Elvis Presley hits of the late fifties. We got to know each other and began dating. She knew that I was a medical student, and she attended Far Eastern University where she studied banking and finance. Her name was Sylvia, and she later became my wife and lifetime partner.

Almost every two weeks I went to see my grandmother who lived in Araneta, just outside metro Manila. I had to take two bus ride to get to her and also say hello to my senile grandfather. My grandmother gave me the money for my tuition, and my job was to accompany my grandfather to go to metro Manila to see movies. I was assigned to take care of him, which I didn't mind because I got to see the movies. The wide-screen CinemaScope theater was in Manila then. I saw every movie shown in CinemaScope and continued until my senior year at the college of medicine. At one point I had to ask the help of a friend in school who had a B.S. in biology to teach me how to start intravenous fluids and perform catheter penile insertion on my grandfather because he was getting incontinent and could not hold his urine. He passed away before my graduation.

In my third year of college, I was informed by my grandmother that money was getting tight and she would let me know more as soon as she could. This bothered me a lot because I knew I could not work as a medical student because my classes were from 8:00 A.M. to 5:00 P.M.

The summer was over, and school started in June. A few months later my grandmother told me that the money problem was imminent I could not concentrate on my studies and failed three subjects. I started looking for work after school hours. I found a job selling credit cards. But credit cards were practically nonexistent in those days, so I had trouble selling those pieces of plastic. I had to think of something else to earn money to pay my tuition as well. I bought an OB-GYN (obstetrics and gynecology) book that we used in school. I outlined each chapter of the book and sought help from my friend in Legarda who owned a school supply. He told me where to buy a used portable mimeographing machine, and he offered to supply the stencil paper and ink on credit. That gave me the incentive to really do the work and at the same time study—a great idea! I was killing two birds with one stone. My girlfriend Sylvia was willing to work with me. Our routine was that I would outline each chapter by long hand and give it to her to be typed. The following day I would correct some errors. I had borrowed an Underwood typewriter from one of my uncles who was a lawyer, and after double-checking the typed manuscript I gave it back to Sylvia with stencil paper. I told her not to make any mistakes because there was no way we could correct it on a stencil paper.

The following day, I would run the stencil paper on the mimeographing machine which was at my beside and run several copies each night to be ready for distribution on the following day at school. This routine went on for about a year and a half. Every day I went to school with two bags in my hands. I went to each classroom and tried to find a student who could sell the outlines for me. I had no difficulty in finding sellers because the commission was fifty cents. The outline was eight to ten pages with old questions and answers from previous exams, and it sold for P 1.50 each. The fifty cent commission went to the seller. Like me, the other students did not have money themselves, and they are anxious and motivated to sell the outline. Every break period I made rounds to collect all the money and take their orders. Boy! They were selling like hot cakes! I was able to open a bank account, pay my tuition, and give my girlfriend gifts that you can't imagine.

In my school, the unwritten rule was that if you reached the third year in medical school, they would never kick you out of school. I failed in three subjects and was branded an irregular student or an Octoberian (graduating in October).I was not the only one in the crowd; there were plenty of Octoberians in my class. Several of them were there for years; we called them professional students. I got to know them very well, and they gave me the old test questions and answers that they had accumulated and saved for years. I mimeographed them and added them to my outlines on the last two or three pages. To my surprise one page of the examination that year was the exact copy of the pages I added to the outline. My business soared like hell. I heard through the grapevine that the dean of the school was investigating the source of the outlines. Nobody turned me in because their business would stop too.

I branched out, doing several outlines on some other subjects, and those went well too. The nice thing about my business was that I was able to study and earn money without leaving school. The OB-GYN book I outlined, I knew by heart, and the knowledge I learned was very useful to me in the years to come. Modesty aside, I can tell you that one could call me a specialist in OB-GYN.

During my rounds to collect and take orders, I noticed that one particular student who had been one of my sellers did not order anything from me on two occasions, while the rest of my sellers were keeping up with their orders. I checked with several classmates of his about whether they had bought outlines from him. They showed me the outlines that came from him. They were the exact copy of my outline; the only difference was that they had been typed with a different typewriter. I told my friends about these guys trying to undermine my business. In our group we had a "slugger" who did the fistfighting for us. He is a general surgeon now like me and is practicing now in Missouri. He told me that he would take care of it. Well, he did. I don't know exactly what happened, but I think he intimidated the head honcho of the other group. I just heard a rumor that they were arguing, and one day the head honcho of the other group brought a gun to school. The word spread like wildfire, and my friend the slugger got out of the school right away. It was not reported to the school or to the police; to us it was an internal matter

their house in San Pablo Laguna, an old, big Spanish house in the middle of the town. The boys never made it to UST, though.

I could feel the friction between my mom and my uncle, and one afternoon my uncle told me he wanted his typewriter back. I told him it was not with me; it was over at Sylvia's house. We went there together, and I gave him the typewriter. I was just thinking to myself, *What kind of uncle is this person? He knows this is my source of income.* I did not say anything, though; anyway, I was in the last few months of my schooling and soon wouldn't have any use for it anymore. That was the last time I saw him. But when I was practicing in St. Petersburg, Florida, I got a call from him. He was working as a waiter in Sacramento, California, and was probably waiting for me to invite him to come to Florida. I interrupted our conversation because I got an emergency call on the other line. I could never forget what he had done to me and to my mother. My mother worked as a dressmaker just to help him to go to school; she only went up to the sixth grade of schooling because she was the firstborn and felt an obligation to send her younger brother to school. I surprised everybody in the family when I became a physician. All my cousins and uncles are lawyers and judges in the Philippines. I guess I am the black sheep of the family.

I had developed a deep bond with my cousins that was shattered by the differences between our elders. We suffered the collateral damage. I missed those guys. The oldest one joined the U.S. Navy, and the one next in age to him married a physician. When I was in New York for a conference, the one who had married a physician and had become an accountant visited me in my hotel with my old friend from Legarda who was working as an orderly in one of the hospitals in New Jersey. We had dinner together and had a good conversation just like old times. I could feel the uneasiness from them because of our different statuses in life. I told them I was still the same guy from Legarda, and my feelings toward them had not changed. They knew I had worked hard to get to where I was and that I still had a sense of humility about where I came from. My accounting friend had a daughter going to school at Columbia University in New York, and he told me that he could not get along with his daughter. I advised him to remember human nature and that kids have a tendency to rebel at a certain age. Being a father he should understand that. I gave them my telephone number and my address in Florida before leaving.

UNIVERSITY OF SANTO TOMAS
PRE - MED

The Quadricentennial Celebration

In the year 2011, the University of Santo Tomas (UST) have reached its 400 years of dedicated service for almost four centuries it has produced saints and martyrs, four presidents of the country, national heroes, leaders, doctors, lawyers and other professionals who have contributed and assumed weighty responsibilities in the Filipino society and church.

The University of Santo Tomas was originally founded by Msgr. Miguel de Benevides, OP on April 28, 1611 in Intramuros, Manila. It was finally elevated from college to a university status by Pope Innocent X. In 1792, students and faculties fought against the invading British army. In recognition to this event King Charles III of Spain conferred the titles from *Loyal* to *Royal* to the university.

Queen Isabella III of Spain ordered UST the only institution for higher learning, the power to govern all Philippine schools. During that time all diplomas were issued by UST.

In 1902, UST was named as a *Pontifical University* by Pope Leo XII.

In 1947, Pope Pius XII declared UST as a *Catholic University of the Philippines.* Due to increasing numbers of enrollees UST prompted to expand and relocated in Sampaloc district. In 1927 the Intramuros campus was officially closed.

The original entrance to the university is the *Arch of the Centuries* ruins facing the main building were part of the original structure created in 1611, while the replica faces the Espana street. Nearby you will find the *Fountain of Wisdom* and the *Fountain of Knowledge.* The end of the lane you will find the *Plaza Mayor*, a park patterned after European Plazas. The square centerpiece is the Benavides Monument dedicated to the school's founder. The bronze statue was made in Paris in 1889 by Tony Noel. The UST main building was the first earthquake resistant structure in the country, engineered by Father Roque Ruano.

During the Japanese occupation of the Philippines UST was used as an internment camp by the Japanese forces in

WW II. The school was closed during that time and reopened after the liberation of Manila by the American forces.

Inside the main building is the Museum of Arts and Sciences which contains permanent displays of Oriental Arts, ethnographic materials, specimens of natural history, 17th to 20th century paintings by Filipino masters. Aside from the main building, there are other venues such as the Beato Angelico gallery, UST chapel, UST archives and Miguel de Benavides Library.

Throughout its nearly 400 years of existence, UST became one of the Philippine attactions for tourist, students and researchers.

UST today, has its mini commercial center containing small snack houses, fast food chain, small shops and restaurant.

To allow more Filipinos to benefit from the quality education that UST has been noted for and true to its mission of the advancement and transmission of knowledge, UST has expanded beyond its campus in Sampaloc, Manila. New satellite of campuses were established in Santa Rosa, Laguna and General Santos in Cotabato City in the southern part of the Philippines.

CLASSMATES COLLEGE OF MEDICINE

CHAPTER 5

Internship

After graduating from the college of medicine, I had to spend one year doing an internship as a prerequisite to getting to use MD after my name. I was assigned to Veterans Administration Hospital in Quezon City which is outside metro Manila. Most of the things I learned there were basic such as starting an intravenous line and other minor things that I was not so enthused about. The volume of paperwork I had to deal with was so much that sometimes I spent the whole day reviewing records. The other interns were just passing their time gambling and fooling around. Once a fire broke out in the interns' quarters, probably from a lit cigarette. I could not take the situation the way it was any longer. I didn't have the luxury of not learning anything like the other interns, who came from well-to-do families.

I went back to the medical school and spoke to the dean. I told him what was happening at the VA hospital.

I explained that I was just wasting my time there and not learning anything. I also informed him that I wanted to be a surgeon like him and that the VA hospital was not the place to learn surgery. He listened to me and transferred me to North General Hospital in metro Manila where the action was. If you wanted to be a surgeon you needed to see major trauma, and the emergency room was the place to be. There was a lot of trauma: gunshot wounds, stabbings, and motor-vehicle accidents, to name a few. You also got to deliver babies sometimes, which I was very comfortable with. The interns usually went with the paramedics in the ambulances whenever there was an emergency call; but the traffic in Manila was just too much, and often by the time we got to our destination, it was too late to do anything.

My first assignment was the emergency room. There were four interns and one emergency room physician supervising us. He tried his best to supervise us, but the volume of patients was so large that we had to work on our own without his input.

There were three medical schools assigned to rotate in that hospital. One of those medical students is now my personal Medicare physician here in Brandon, Florida. There were few incidents that stayed in my long-term memory that I cannot forget. One patient I saw was a young man whose right wrist was bleeding; the tendons were sticking out like spaghetti. We surgeons call this "spaghetti wrist," as the situation and injury imply. It took me more than two hours to repair the damage in the ER under local anesthesia. In the wrist, there are two layers of tendons. One layer is a superficial set of tendons, and the other group is the deep tendon clusters. I started with deep ones first and worked my way up. The story the man told me was that he was trying to block a stab by a Balisong (butterfly knife) with his hand during the fight. I gave him instructions to keep the dressing clean and dry, to not move his fingers for two weeks, and to follow up in the clinic. I never saw him again.

The other unforgettable incident was this: another male patient came in with a blood-soaked towel covering his penis. When I asked him what had happened, he said, "Doc, I just had a circumcision done by a friend, but it won't stop bleeding."

Theoretically, a backyard circumcision can be done by anybody with a shaving blade or a sharp knife. The sharp end of the blade is inserted inside the skin of the penis (prepuce) with the sharp end of the blade facing up and is then hit with a piece of wood. The only problem with this procedure is that if you are not aware of the vein (dorsal vein) running on the top skin the patient will bleed like hell. I told the man to lay down on a nearby stretcher, and he complied. I took care of it by suturing the bleeder and finishing the job.

My next rotation was surgery. The intern was the first assistant most of the time; otherwise he or she would be the third assistant, holding the retractors. The bloodiest surgery of them all was the suprapubic prostatectomy (surgical removal of the prostate gland). We seldom do it now; instead we perform a trans-urethral resection (TUR) whereby we remove the prostate gland piece by piece through a scope. We did a lot of hernia repair and the occasional nephrectomy (removal of the kidney).

As an intern we didn't receive stipends, and we had to pay for our internship; so we had to devise ways to make some money. Pharmaceutical company representative called on interns while we were working to try to introduce us to the new medicines and give us samples of them. We sold the samples we had accumulated to a pharmacy across the street from the hospital; we called this "sample selling." Every day the pharmacy was expecting us, cash in hand; that became our spending money.

My next rotation was in a public maternity clinic. This was my area of expertise. I delivered a lot of babies, and three of them had anencephaly (no skull bones). In each case I first thought I was delivering a breach presentation (the baby emerging butt first) because I could feel something soft; but this turned out to be the head with no skull bones, and of course the baby was dead. In those days, ultrasound was not in existence; it only became available in the seventies when I was practicing in Florida. The technology works through bouncing sound waves like a submarine sonar. You send a sound signal, and it bounces back thus mapping out images of what is inside the uterus. It can recognize fetal abnormalities and early detachment of the placenta and can locate the placenta as well. I assisted in a lot of C-section, hysterectomies (removal of the uterus), and so on.

The other rotation was for communicable diseases in San Lazaro Hospital. There I got to draw blood from patients with active tuberculosis. In those days we administered pure oxygen, not by a nasal cannula like what you see in the hospital today but with a plastic-covered tent over the patient. Because of this constant minimal exposure, I developed some sort of immunity to tuberculosis that showed up as a positive tuberculin test on me.

Another part of our job was to screen women "of ill repute." They came to the clinic on a regular basis to be tested for venereal diseases. We did a lot of internal examination and Pap smears, taking sample of their vaginal fluids for microscopic analysis. Some enterprising intern kept a list of those whose tests came back negative, I guess for future use.

Another rotation was in Victoriano Luna (or V. Luna) General Hospital, which was mainly for Filipino veterans of the war. Here I learned about the radioisotope of iodine for thyroid and cervical cancers. One of the interns got to be the sidekick of a gynecologist and carried around his ten-pound lead box. I utilized my time to learn on every rotation. On this rotation I learned how to read an EKG (Electrocardiogram), and I have used that skill many times while in the States.

A strange incident happened in V. Luna Hospital while I was off duty. The news reported that a sergeant shot an intern for a gambling debt. The story in the paper was murky, and I don't know if there was a court-martial or not. It did not last very long in the news.

I graduated November 7, 1964, a year and a half late. During our internships, we studied for the Philippine board. I took the examination and passed it with an average of 81 percent. Our names were published in the newspaper, which could be quite embarrassing if you failed because everybody read the papers. I was granted a license to practice medicine and surgery in the Philippines and got MD affixed to my name at last. In fact I still have the original license with me to the present day.

For those who wanted further training, the United States was the place to be. You had to pass an examination given by the Educational Council for Foreign Medical Graduates (ECFMG), which was based in Evanston, Illinois. You were allowed only two years of post-graduate courses. The test consisted of two parts. One part was an English examination, and the other was the medical part. We didn't have problems with the English part of the examination because we had been taught English since primary school, and we were only allowed to speak English in medical school.

English was our second language. When the Americans came in the early 1900s, they changed the school system and it patterned after the U.S. system. If you want to travel to the Philippines, you can get by using only English. Tagalog, our national language, is mainly spoken in the main island of Luzon. We have eighteen dialects, and each of our seven thousand islands has its own means of communication.

Some of our interns went to Europe, specifically Sweden. The reason remains a puzzle to me—maybe because they didn't have to take the ECFMG exams or maybe there was no time limitation on their stay as there was in the United States. One thing I know is that the Swedish girls, blonde and blue-eyed, kept knocking on their doors with bottles of wine. What man could say no to that? I don't know about their post-graduate studies, and I never heard anymore of what happened to them.

During my internship I started going through each subject in medicine superficially just to remember the salient points on each subject. There were quite a number of them. I had been dating my girlfriend for about three years, and I promised her I would take her to the United States to start our new life together in a distant land, the land of the free! We did and had four children born in the States who were all educated and have become professionals. They are married now and living successful lives. We have six Eurasian grandchildren.

CHAPTER 6

Educational Council for Foreign Medical Graduates (ECFMG)

After my Philippine board examination, I applied for the ECFMG examination. It took a while to get the response from Evanston, Illinois. A lot of us took the examination in a big stadium in Manila. The English part of the examination was the easy part; the second part is a lot tricky. Trying to understand the questions was difficult. We were not trained to take that kind of examination, which used Moore's type of questioning, in which, for example if statement 1 and statement 3 in a list of statements were correct, the answer would be A, but if statements 1, 2, and 3 were correct, the answer would be B. Trying to figure out the questions themselves was hard enough regardless of how knowledgeable the test taker was in medicine.

A few months later I got the report and received a grade of 74 percent. I needed 75 percent to pass; I had failed. A lot of my classmates passed the exam knowing that I was a little better than them. I was very curious about how they had done it; low and behold, they had called their friends in the United States and asked them what subjects to read and study. After the examination, I knew more or less what to study for the next time around.

My girlfriend and I went to church almost every week to pray to St. Jude for help and guidance. All my classmates who passed eventually went to the United States. Boy was I heartbroken! A few years later when I was in New York, I heard that all my classmates who had gone to the USA were sent home after two years of training. Some of them went to the Virgin Islands, and some went to Canada.

At that time, the Vietnam War was going on, and there were a lot of demonstrations against it. Many American doctors were in Vietnam during the war, so the United States needed doctors at home to fill the gap. President Lyndon Johnson, I believe, issued a presidential proclamation that all foreign doctors under training did not have to go home. They could stay in the United States if they wished. Now I realized that my failure in taking the ECFMG examination was a *blessing in disguise*. It looks like somebody up there was watching over me.

I went to New Jersey and applied for citizenship; I swore an oath of allegiance many years later in Tampa, Florida, while in practice.

Again, I sent another application, took the examination again, and got a passing grade. So I had to search for a place in the United States for my training in surgery, but I also had to repeat the internship again as a requirement. It so happened that Sylvia's dad had a client who was a controller in a hospital in Saginaw, Michigan. I gave him all the documents that were needed, and in turn he gave them to the medical director of the hospital when he went back to the States. The administrator of the hospital sent me a letter of acceptance. St. Luke's Hospital was a good hospital for doing internships because there were no residents. We interns did all the work of the hospital physicians.

I replaced my old classmate from North General Hospital, and another classmate was training in internal medicine in the neighboring hospital. He had to leave because his two years were about to expire, so he went to Canada to finish his training. When President Johnson signed the presidential decree, my classmate went to San Antonio, Texas, and took anesthesiology.

My girlfriend and I were very excited and made preparations for our departure for the United States. I had promised Sylvia that I would take her with me because of the hard work she had done for me when I was out of money during my third year of schooling. I made arrangements for the two of us through a travel agency on a "fly now and pay later" deal. The travel agency arranged the visa, passport, and itinerary; we were to stop over in Hong Kong and Japan.

My girlfriend and I got married in Sampaloc Church on December 27, 1965, in a very simple wedding with my friends as witnesses. After the wedding her sister invited us for a coffee and cookies. I paid the priest fifty dollars for the ceremony. We were all broke during that time and could not afford a lavish wedding. That was only for rich folks! I promised myself that I would give her a big fiftieth wedding anniversary celebration (without telling her, though, since I thought we might not still be alive).

Before I left for the States, I had a long talk with my grandmother. Our conversation has stayed with me all these years, and I fulfilled every promise I made to her. She told me not to worry about her; she said that if she died and I could not afford to go home that I should not worry about it. She emphasized that I should take care of my mom and dad and my two sisters as long as I lived. In the Philippines we don't have Social Security. Since coming to the United States I have been sending money to my mom and dad for eighteen years non-stop. I was their "Social Security" irrespective of my expenses in the United States.

My grandmother died when I was in training, and as she predicted, I didn't have the money to go home. My uncle Manolo sent me photos. It was a sad moment for me. It took me a while to understand how she viewed the world. She was a very practical woman. She knew that we lived in a male-dominated society, and she saw women as subservient to the male gender. She let her daughters work instead of attend school so that my uncles could be professionals. I believe that's an old-school way of thinking, and that old-school thinking is still happening today. The Catholic Church is a very good example of that, as well as our government system; both are ruled by men.

All the teachings and advice she gave me stayed with me, developed my character, and molded me into the person I am now. As a leader you should understand the thinking of the people under you, the scope of their capabilities and their philosophy of life. Reasoning and persuasion—not imposing your will upon others—is what I call leadership.

Wisdom is defined as knowledge and experience combined. I would add to that definition common sense. We , the United States as a nation occasionally were deprived of this virtue. We were too enthused with details that we missed the whole picture of who we were as a society of different nations.

UST 1964 DINNER DANCE
MANILA HOTEL

1965 MANILA INTERNATIONAL AIRPORT

CHAPTER 7

St. Luke's Hospital, Saginaw, Michigan

Two days after our wedding Sylvia and I embarked on our journey to the United States. Our families and close friends were at the airport to say good-bye. My uncle Manolo gave me two hundred dollars for pocket money. My friend tried to give me salted duck eggs, a Chinese delicacy, but I told him I could not take it because U.S. customs were strict. I just said thank you.

We had to stop in Hong Kong to have our topcoats made to order for us in preparation for the winter weather in Michigan. It took only twenty-four hours for them to make the coats. Nowadays it is not like that anymore. We stopped over in Japan and took a straight flight to Chicago as our port of entry. Of course going through customs was a pain in the neck. From Chicago we took a prop plane to Saginaw. It was about three o'clock in the morning by then, and we took a taxi to the controller's house and slept there overnight.

The hospital had a house ready for us, and we moved in the following day. My classmate, Celso Samaniego, came and visited us and took us to a grocery store. Those of us with last names beginning with S were grouped together in one classroom, so he was really my classmate. And, by the way, he paid for the groceries!

On my first day of work I got to meet the administrator and the medical director, Dr. Young. I met the rest of the interns and my Filipino doctor friend from North General Hospital in Manila. My first few weeks were a little bit difficult for me because they could not understand my so-called Filipino English. We don't have a long A sound in our pronunciation; so instead we used short As. But I corrected my mistake right away. My experience told me that the American interns looked down on me for being a foreigner. It's possible that I was paranoid or had a complex, but I don't think that was all there was to it. I could just feel it, but, being a rookie, I did nothing .

Every Sunday morning, over breakfast, all the interns and the medical director had a short clinicopathological conference (CPC). The case presenter had to pick a case that would be presented for each of us to make a diagnosis. Usually at the back of the *New England Journal of Medicine* there would be a problematic case, and it was our job to make a diagnosis. We bet fifty-cent antes on the table, and whoever made the correct diagnosis got the pot. My training in UST was to diagnose illnesses just by pure physical examinations, X-rays, and patient histories alone without the benefit of any special laboratory information. In four or five consecutive Sundays, I got the diagnosis (and or close to it), depending of which organ of the body was involved. I took the pots on those days.

The other interns got suspicious and went to the library to investigate. They met with the librarian and asked her why I was always getting the diagnosis. The librarian showed the interns the rows of shelves containing the journals from wall to wall and asked them, "Do you think he can cheat with all these rows of journals?" The group didn't say anything—just turned and left. She told me about the incident when I visited the library. From then on and thereafter, things changed for me for the better.

At St. Luke's Hospital, the general practitioner did the tonsillectomies (removal of the tonsils) in kids. They knew that I wanted to be a surgeon, so guess who ended up doing the tonsillectomies? Yours truly. The GP also delivered babies. I assisted one good-looking GP who resembled the actor Robert Taylor. His patient had very poor uterine contractions. I suggested stimulating the posterior fornix of the vagina (the back wall behind the cervix). Remember, I was supposed to be an OB-GYN specialist! He did what I suggested and out came the baby! He asked me later where I learned the technique. I answered, "From a book."

The word spread around with the nurses, and every time they had problems they somehow learned to page me. And on top of all that I got to do all the circumcisions of all the male babies every week.

On one occasion, one of the attending surgeons suggested that we go bowling. Our bowling balls in the Philippines are small, just about the size of a grapefruit with no holes in them. What I saw this first time was a ball as big as my head and with three holes in it. I asked my co-intern quietly, "What are those holes for?" He demonstrated that one hole was for the thumb and the other two were for the index and middle fingers. I figured out what to do to shoot a straight ball. The fulcrum was in my shoulder; and I had to keep my wrist and elbow steady and point my thumb where I wanted the ball to go. They let me practice a few times to get familiar with it. On the first game, I got six strikes in a row. They had trouble trying to compute my score. There were no computers in those days, as you know.

A few months went by and I bought my first car, a Mustang with a stick shift. In the Philippines I was well domesticated. I had learned how to type in a vocational school and had also learned how to drive by going to a driving school. The school taught me about the engine, transmission, and brakes, and about the car's mechanisms and functions. My uncle Felipe let me borrow his jeepney, and I practiced my driving skills in the streets of Manila. You think driving in New York is bad? The rules are not obeyed in Manila. My driving instructor took me to a bridge in Manila and taught me how to balance the clutch and gas pedal on the uphill incline of the bridge. When I was in New York, I had no problem driving in Manhattan and its boroughs.

My wife was in her third trimester of pregnancy. She called one night while I was on duty at St. Luke's and told me that she was having pains. I asked her how close together the pains were, and she said, "It is not regular—off and on." I knew then that it was just a Braxton-Hicks contraction (false labor). To keep her mind at ease, I asked her to walk to the hospital and sleep in my room, which had two single beds. In the morning she walked back home, which was just across the street. I got summoned to the controller's office later, and he asked me what my wife was doing in my room. I told him about the pains she was having and said that it just to ease her nerves since this was her first baby. Apparently, while we were sleeping, an intern had walked in to get his lab coat and had seen us sleeping.

A few weeks went by. Her due date was around the second week of December. There was a big snowstorm that particular day, and she was reporting to me how close her contractions were. When she told me they were every ten minutes, I told her to dress and said I would pick her up. We got into the maternity ward and called the obstetrician. I examined her and did an internal exam. The baby's head was engaged already in the pelvis, and her cervix was dilated about 3 centimeters. I immediately called the OB and told him my findings. He said, "I am on my way." I knew the streets had at least five inches of snow and thought the doctor might not be able to get there in time. I stayed with Sylvia, and a nurse continued to monitor her contractions and fetal heartbeat. The frequency of contraction was getting shorter and shorter. I did another exam, and she was about six centimeters dilated. In obstetrics, the rule of thumb is that in most primigravida (first pregnancy), it usually takes time to deliver. But there is always an exception to the rule—and on that day, it was my wife. We took her to the delivery room and prepped her for delivery while waiting for her doctor. I immediately did a pudendal block on each side of the labia (local anesthesia) to ease her pain during delivery. Right after the block, she began pushing hard. The baby's head was crowning already (that is, the baby's head was starting to show), but the doctor was not in yet. So I delivered my first baby, and she was a big girl! As soon as the baby was out, the doctor walked in, and he delivered the placenta. Was I scared? Not a bit! My wife was just like any other woman I had helped deliver a baby. As a physician I developed a shield from my emotion in doing my job. Remember, I was supposed to be an OB-GYN specialist! I knew somebody up there was ahead of me. I said to myself, "Of all the books I could have picked to outline in college, why did I pick the OB-GYN book?" I now knew the reason;

somebody up there had known all along, and now I knew as well. There is always a reason for whatever happens here on earth; we may not know it at the time, though—only God knows.

After the delivery was all over, I felt the drain in my system. We named our baby Christine. She grew up and went to the University of Texas A&M School of Architecture and now has two girls of her own. She now lives in Alpharetta, Georgia.

Saginaw General Hospital

I started my internship on January 1, 1966, in the middle of the training program. I had to talk to the medical director to ask if I could stay six more months to have a fresh start in my residency for July of the next year. It would be difficult for me to find an opening in any surgical program right in the middle. I had a good six months to look for a surgical residency program. I applied first to Baylor University where the famous heart surgeon Dr. Michael Debakey was the chief of surgery. I never got a response. I applied to some other hospitals, but they had no openings. I ended up across the street at Saginaw General Hospital and spent my first year of surgical residency there. Boy, did they love having me as their resident! It was not too bad. (I had thought it would be.) It was affiliated with the University of Michigan, Ann Arbor.

I learned the elective aspects of surgery, but they were all non-emergency cases. I was taught well and learned how to take my time without outside pressure and do a good job. I learned the art and science of Surgery. The only thing missing from the cases at Saginaw General Hospital were emergency surgeries.

I spoke to my wife and said that we would have to move. We had been able to save about seven hundred dollars, but that was not good enough to go to either Canada or the Virgin Islands. I could not moonlight in Saginaw to save money. I kept sending out applications for my second year of residency in general surgery. On January 5,1968 my second child, Cheryl, was born. She became a nurse (BSN) with a master's degree. She died of breast cancer, a highly malignant non-estrogen-responding tumor. May her soul rest in peace. She was thirty-eight when she passed away, and she left two children, Libby and Bootchie my first grandchildren. Of all the years I have practiced General Surgery, most breast tumors I have encountered have been estrogen positive, which means they respond to anti-estrogenic drugs. It is difficult for a parent to lose a child too soon. It was totally devastating. Children are supposed to cry over their parents; parents should not have to cry over their own children. I loved her very dearly.

One day I received a letter from Jamaica Hospital in New York, which said they had an opening for a second-year surgical resident. I grabbed the opportunity and sent for a contract. They also provided housing for the resident, and I would be able to moonlight to save more money just in case our two years were up and we would have to leave soon.

We had a two-week vacation, so we went driving to see Mount Rushmore. On our way back, close to home, the transmission just dropped off the car! As soon as it was fixed, I traded the car in for a Pontiac Bonneville. It was a much bigger car and had room for my two children. It could also haul trailers. I flew to New York for an interview and found out that their ER was busy with lots of emergency surgeries. I signed the contract and went back to Saginaw. On the last week of June we packed our belongings in a U-Haul trailer and drove to New York. Prior to that, while I was still living in Michigan, I drove to New York to visit my classmates who had gone ahead of me. They were preparing to go back home because their two-year training was almost over. I asked if they could show me around, but they said that they could not because they were afraid of driving in New York. I had a map of New York City that I had gotten from AAA. I drove them to Battery Park in the southern end of Manhattan to take a ferry to see the Statue of Liberty, which they had not seen either.

On my way to New York I was stopped by a highway trooper on the Pennsylvania Turnpike for speeding. I was taken to court and paid a fine of two hundred dollars from my AAA card. I eventually paid AAA at a later date. That was my first and last speeding ticket.

As I said before, New York traffic was nothing compared to traffic in Manila, where no rules applied. I drove back to Michigan after the trip.

That summer, a Filipino doctor, an old-timer who was married to an American woman, told me that he had not eaten *lechon* (a Spanish word for roasted pig) for quite sometime. I told him that I could make it for him on my weekend off. He provided me with an eighty-pound pig, cleaned with the internal organs taken out, a wooden pole about eight feet long, and bags of charcoal. In his backyard I dug a four-foot-by-six-foot hole that was a foot deep. It took me four or five hours to cook the pig, and we took turns rotating the pig on the pole. When we had finished, the skin was red and crispy, and everybody had a good time eating.

CHAPTER 8

Jamaica Hospital, Queens, New York

Sylvia and I left Saginaw in the early morning hours with our two kids and a U-Haul trailer hitched to my Bonneville. We drove along the Pennsylvania Turnpike through New Jersey and crossed the Verrazano Narrows Bridge, heading toward JFK Airport. Jamaica Hospital was just north of the airport on Van Wyck Expressway. It was beginning to get dark when we arrived, and we parked close to the hospital. I went inside and looked for the nurse supervisor or the head of the maintenance department. The maintenance guy showed me where we would be living. As soon as we turned on the lights, we saw that the house was infested with cockroaches all over the floor. I told the maintenance guy that I had two kids with me and there was no way I could live there. He made a few phone calls, and we were directed to a Kew Gardens apartment complex a mile north of the hospital. It was a Jewish community, and the three-bedroom apartment was clean. We got ourselves settled and checked out the neighborhood. It was a quiet and peaceful place. We found the bank nearby and the grocery store. They are both walking distance from our apartment.

I reported to the director of surgery, and he gave my assignment and call schedule. We were divided into two groups, each with an intern and four surgical residents. Each group had to rotate every other day and every other weekend. I did the rotation for three years and barely saw my family. My wife was the one taking care of the children. I was moonlighting on a call schedule at a nearby hospital. There were plenty of those in New York, and I got what I wanted: more bucks and more experience with trauma in the ER. Boy, was it hard work! If our team was on call, we would work the whole night. We could forget about sleep; the most we could do was take a two- or three-hour nap. Stabbings, shooting, blunt traumas—you name it, we saw it. About four or five cases of major trauma a night. I got sick and tired of opening bellies. I have to talked to the interns who wants to be a surgeon and I will be very glad to teach him. On my off hours, I worked in the hospital's ER to earn more bucks.

It was around 1968 or '69 when President Lyndon B. Johnson signed a proclamation that all foreign doctors under training did not have to go home and could apply for immigrant status in the United States. Immediately I went to work and filed my naturalization papers in New Jersey, where the U.S. Immigration and Naturalization Service office was located. I realized then that my failure on the ECFMG examination was a blessing in disguise. I guess somebody up there likes me. It took many years to process, and I finally took the oath in Tampa across the Howard Franklin Bridge from St. Petersburg, Florida, in 1983.

New York is a cosmopolitan city. The group of residents I worked with were from all over the world. We had Koreans, East Indians, and residents from Latin America. I thought my English was bad, but compared to those guys, I was an Englishman! We had a little trouble communicating because of our different accents. I was chosen to present a case in a conference of colorectal surgeons in Manhattan. I was the last presenter and was scheduled to speak after dinner. The residents before me had presented statistics with all figures and numbers. I saw the attending doctors beginning to fall asleep. So when I began, I opened my case by saying, "Doctors, I just hope you are all awake!" Everybody started laughing. I presented my case, and everybody was attentive.

After a year in Kew Gardens, they moved our family to a vacant house near the hospital.

The director of surgery assigned me to handle the blood-gas machine, which measured the oxygen concentration of blood. It was difficult to calibrate the machine, and I had to do it every morning. Now the blood gases are measured in laboratories by technicians.

Working and moonlighting in New York exposed me to different strains of bacteria and viruses. I got sick for two weeks and isolated myself in a small room at home. I was seen by a specialist from John Hopkins Hospital and could not diagnose my sickness. I had terrible headaches, high fevers, and a rash all over my body. I had to call my coresident to give me a shot of one hundred milligrams of Demerol just to ease the headaches (meningismus: inflammation of the lining of the brain). The dose of Demerol was enough to knock out a horse. I finally got better and started researching my sickness. My conclusion was that it was a variant of scarlet fever. I had all the symptoms including PVCs (premature ventricular beats) that show on EKGs occasionally because scarlet fever affects the heart. I thought that was the end of me! It took many years for those PVCs to go away. Life insurance companies kept turning me down because of it, and I had no life insurance for years. It finally went away when I was in practice, and then I was able to get a life insurance.

On November 7, 1969, my third child, a boy, was born in Jamaica Hospital. He graduated as salutatorian at Shorecrest Preparatory School at age sixteen. He was promoted several times in his primary and school years. He went to the Wharton School at the University of Pennsylvania and was out of college at age twenty. He worked for a Japanese bank in New York and then with Ralph Lauren and two other clothing companies. He went to Harvard Business School and received his MBA in a year and a half. He speaks five languages. Ralph Lauren assigned him to Hong Kong to represent the company and manage the business over there. He was back and forth for several months between New York and Hong Kong. They finally got him an apartment in Hong Kong where he is living right at this moment as I am writing this book.

In my fourth year of residency, my sister Luzviminda and her husband immigrated to the United States and stayed with us for a while. She worked in the hospital, and her husband worked for the United Parcel Service.

I knew then that the general surgery specialty alone would not be enough to live by. My experience told me that there were a lot of general surgeons who were starving. They were in the ER all the time, hanging out and waiting for cases—it was that bad.

I knew one attending surgeon in Jamaica Hospital who had a sub-specialty in hand surgery. He got his training at Wayne State University in Detroit. I started working on that right away by getting in touch with the director of the program. Before proceeding to Detroit, I had to buy a house for my sister and my parents. A few months before I had sent some money to them so they could visit us with my baby sister Inicita. My sister luzviminda have five kids, but they are still in the Philippines, as nobody in New York would rent you an apartment for that big a family. I was able to save a little over four thousand because of my moonlighting jobs. We found a three-bedroom house in South Ozone Park, an Italian neighborhood located between the Belmont Race track and the hospital. This was the first house that the Soriano family ever owned. I just gave it to my sister. The house was about twenty years old and needed some fixing. I bought them a refrigerator at Sears and a few beds and furnishings. Around the corner was a bus stop that would take riders to Jamaica Hospital. They didn't have a car because nobody knew how to drive. But you didn't need a car in New York;. Public transportation was easily available and accessible; you just had to know which bus or subway to take.

For the meantime I was busy communicating with Wayne State University for my hand fellowship program. Usually it would take several months to prepare.

My parents and Inicita came, and now they had a house to go to. We were busy showing them the tourist sights in New York such as Rockefeller Center, Radio City Music Hall, the Statue of Liberty, and Ellis Island. We even took them to see Niagara Falls.

JAMAICA HOSPITAL SURGICAL RESIDENTS
NEW YORK 1970

CHAPTER 9

Hand Surgery Fellowship
Wayne State University, Detroit

My first attempt to drive back to Detroit was a failure. The Bonneville transmission was beginning to get hot and started to burn oil; my U-Haul trailer was too heavy. I returned it and rented a small truck instead. We had accumulated some furniture because of my growing family. I took my dad with me for a ride to Michigan, and he helped me unload the stuff. I rented a small three-bedroom house (a freestanding apartment) in Royal Oak on Fourteenth Mile Road exit. We set the family's things inside, ready to be unpacked. I showed my dad where to buy the groceries and left him there to watch the house. I returned the U-Haul truck and flew back to New York to fetch my family and drive back to Detroit. After getting settled in Royal Oak, I sent my father back to New York.

There were five of us fellows in the hand surgery program.

We came from various specialties. Our call schedule was once a week. Compared to the call schedule in New York, this was heaven for me. This time I moonlighted in only one place, an Industrial Clinic set up for workman's compensation patients. I stayed in the fellowship for the whole year, instead of just six months. I was in no hurry to get out because I was earning big bucks from the Industrial Clinic. I took my time looking for a place to practice. An attending in St. Luke's Hospital told me to practice where I wanted to live because if I got stuck in the place at least I would like it. The attending said not to worry about the money; it would come. I aimed for the Sunbelt states.

There was one particular surgeon who never gave the fellows any surgeries to do. All you could do was assist him. We booked a case together. When we were about to start the case he stood up and told me, "If you have any problems, I will be in the coffee room." And then he left! The anesthesiologist looked me in the eye and murmured, "He trusts you, Doc!"

In another instance the head of the department scheduled a case for an island pedicle graft, a very delicate surgery. A full thickness of the skin and fat with its blood supply including the nerve is taken from a normal finger and transplanted to either an index finger or thumb for sensation. Usually the donor finger is the ring finger. There were two fellows assigned to the case. While the two of us were waiting for him, he showed up in the room and told us, "Go ahead, fellas.

I will be in the doctors' room if you need me." We looked at each other, astonished. It took me two hours to finish the case. The follow-up was done by my assistant, also a general surgery trainee. He called me from the office while I was in the OR.

He asked, "Carlos, is the graft viable and alive?"

I said, "Thank you for the courtesy."

I learned a lot doing reconstructive work (plastic surgery). For example if someone was missing a thumb from an accident or injury, I could transfer the index finger to be the thumb, and the middle finger would act as the index finger. The function of the thumb and index finger is 40 percent of the hand's function. The rest of the fingers function mainly as hooks. It is important to restore the function of the thumb and index finger for finer point of movements and grasping.

During my weekends off I flew back and forth from Michigan to Texas and Florida, places where there was no snow. I concentrated on Florida. When I was in New York I received an IRS refund of 360 dollars, big bucks in those days. I drove with the family all the way down to Miami. I saw the palm trees and blue water and was sold on Florida right away. I thought, *This is the place!* I took the flex examination for licenses. It covered most of the states, so I became licensed in New York, Michigan, Texas, and Florida. I flew to Beaumont, Texas, and the offer there was irresistible. I could work in the ER, and whatever patients I wanted I could have, along with any cash collected in the ER. The last stop on my trip was St. Petersburg, Florida. I crossed the Howard Franklin Bridge and saw the beautiful water and waterfront homes with docks in the backyard for boats.

Working in the emergency room is a good way to check out a community and find out about the people who live there. I met Dr. Frank Norton who was the chief of emergency medicine in Palms of Pasadena Hospital. He was an engineer before he became a medical doctor. He was also a New Yorker, but he had studied medicine in Milan, Italy. I told him of my plans to open a surgical practice eventually. He told me that he could use me in the ER at Palms of Pasadena Hospital and also at Lake Seminole Hospital. Once that was settled, my next step was to find an apartment. I found one at the southern end of St. Petersburg on Pinellas Point Drive. When I got back to Michigan, I told Sylvia that I had found a place. I have already saved about thirty thousand dollars, and I had two cars—a Corvette and a Ford Thunderbird.

Another son, Chad was born in Detroit on August 5, 1971. He finished high school in St. Petersburg and went to college at SMU (Southern Methodist University) a private school in Dallas, Texas. After school he worked for Channel 13 for many years, and he now works for a group of lawyers taking deposition videos. He married a dentist, and they have two children, Maddy and Jude. He lives right across the street from my wife and me, and my wife babysits them and picks them up after school. My son-in-law also lives in my neighborhood with Libby and Bootchie. Once in a while they stay with us. Their mother is my daughter who died of breast cancer three years ago. Libby will be in high school in the fall of 2010. That indicates the length of time Sylvia has been taking care of the grandchildren.

The only grandchildren she could not take care of were Christine's two girls, Ally and Zoe. They live in Alpharetta, Georgia. Christine takes care of them and had to quit her job because of the children. She has been able to teach them very well. She is married to a blond blue-eyed guy of Norwegian ancestry; their children are of pure Eurasian blood. There is a doctor in San Antonio, Texas, who traces the accomplishment of the Eurasian kids and has come to the conclusion that they are brighter than the rest of the kids in school.

Christine is really doing a good job with her kids. Ally's school wanted to advance her to the fourth grade from first grade because her reading and math were way above the average level for kids her age. Christine sent me an oil painting made by Ally, and we were astonished. Christine was a good swimmer when she was in high school. She sent Ally for swimming lessons, and Ally won several trophies in a swimming competition. Ally is a brunette, but Zoe is blond. I call her Blondie. Zoe is already having similar success as well; she is excellent in school just like her sister.

CHAPTER 10

St. Petersburg, Florida, 1973

When we moved to St. Pete, I drove the Corvette down first and left it in Dr. Norton's backyard. I flew back to Michigan to pick up the family, again with the use of a U-Haul trailer. Interstate I-75 took us to Florida from Michigan in a straight shot. I took my time driving to Florida because of the four kids. As soon as I crossed Howard Franklin Bridge, I made a wrong turn and headed north to Clearwater. I recognized the problem immediately and turned around and went south to Pinellas Point Drive where the Puerto Bello apartments were located. I had signed the papers for a three-bedroom apartment before I left for Michigan. I showed my wife around, taking her to the school, grocery store, and bank.

I worked in various emergency rooms at local hospitals including Bayfront Medical Center, Edward White Hospital, St. Petersburg General Hospital, Palms of Pasadena Hospital, and Lake Seminole Hospital. Within a year I built my first house in the Maximo Moorings and Broadwater area. The house had four bedrooms with a screen enclosure, a swimming pool, and a dock on my seawall for my boat. I bought a used Reinell twenty-eight-foot boat to start with. I docked it right behind my house. It had its own bathroom and a small galley with beds. The family and friends had fun with it.

My uncle Manolo and his wife visited me while we were in the Broadwater area, probably just to check me out if I was doing okay. He was the one who gave me two hundred dollars for pocket money at the Manila airport. He owned a tannery business with his wife in the Philippines. My grandmother, while I was in college in the Philippines, had told me that some of my tuition came from him. I didn't know if it is the truth or not because I knew that my grandmother wanted me to stay close to him. Since I was a kid, I have been a very proud person; I don't usually ask favors from anybody. I don't know if it is just my character or just plain nonsense. In any case, I took my uncle and his wife for a boat ride and showed them the St. Pete area. They finally went back home and told my relatives that I was just doing fine.

A few months later I opened my office in the Seminole area just north, in a suburb of St. Pete. Dr. Norton also opened his office for general practice in the same office complex. Dr. Walsh from Saginaw also had an office in the same area. He was one of my attending doctors at St. Luke's Hospital in Saginaw during my internship. What a small world! I wondered whether it was my luck or just a coincidence. Again, I thought maybe I was meant to be in the place where I was. Dr. Norton kept me busy with my surgical practice.

While in Broadwater I started with my new hobby: old car restoration. This was big time compared to my hobby while I was in Legarda, building model airplanes. I was driving on St. Pete beach when I saw an old 1959 MG TF. I spoke to the driver and found out that he had come from California and was new in the area. I asked him if he is willing to sell his car. He said yes, and I paid him four thousand dollars for the car in cash. I took the car to Pinellas Park where small shops are located. I found somebody who would dismantle the car and paint it inside and out. I changed the color from British racing green to yellow. I had it reupholstered with a matching top and a new wood instrument panel. I changed the tires to white sidewalls, and by the time I was done it looked immaculate. I ordered from Herrings Magazine for antique cars. My second car was a 1960 Morgan. Would you believe it had four disc brakes! That car has a belt on the hood. I did the same restoration that I had done on the first one. Every time there was an antique car show, I entered the two cars. I got a lot of first place and second place trophies. I still have their pictures with me now.

Next door to our house was a vacant lot; I should have taken the advice of my uncle Manolo and bought the lot.

Somebody else bought the lot and decided to build a house on that vacant lot. One night, a Filipino doctor came to have dinner with us. Chad, my youngest, was five or six years old. All of a sudden, he was gone—nowhere to be found. We looked around in the water by the seawall, and finally my friend found him on the roof of the house they were building next door. The contractor had left a ladder, and Chad had climbed up on the roof. My friend immediately climbed up and took him down. I told the contractor the following day. He was sorry about it and glad that no injury had occurred.

A few months later, I bought a small motor home because I was planning to take the family all over the United States and I also wanted to see the country for myself. I planned my trip very well; we would take the lower corridor highway (I-10) to Las Vegas and proceed north and take the northern highway on our way back. We took the trip while the kids were on their summer vacation. We passed by Austin, Texas, to pick up my Texas license and went to San Antonio to see the Riverwalk. San Antonio was a small city then. We headed for Vegas and saw lots of scenery along the way. We parked behind the area for campers behind the Circus Circus Casino. It was hot: 110 degrees. I believe, though I may be mistaken, that Las Vegas in the seventies was still controlled by the Mafia. Big hotels did not exist that time. We stayed a few days and headed north toward the northern corridors of highway. We saw the Grand Tetons just north of Vegas,

Mount Rushmore in the Dakotas, and of course Wild Wood where Wild Bill Hickock and Calamity Jane were buried. We proceeded east to St. Louis, Missouri, and took a trip up to the Gateway Arch. My kids called it the McDonald Arch. I told them it was supposed to be a gateway to the West. I can't forget to mention that we passed through Flagstaff, Arizona (and went to a bank because I had run out of cash) and then proceeded to Grand Canyon. We stayed overnight and drove again the following morning. We stayed mostly in the campgrounds with water and a waste hookup. Once in a while we stayed in a hotel to take proper showers. On our way back home we stopped by the Smoky Mountains in Gatlinburg. With four kids behind me in the motor home, I almost went bananas! I will never do that again. A few months later I sold the motor home.

My Jewish neighbor, who lived two houses down, mentioned when we were jogging together that he knew somebody who was trying to sell a corporate boat. Because it was a corporate boat, nobody used it that much. I went to look at the boat, which was docked at Maximo Moorings around the corner where all the big boats were docked. Some owners lived on the boat, and at first I could not figure out why—to avoid property taxes! I had not been aware of such a thing before.

The boat, made by Chris Craft, was a thirty-three-foot yacht with a full galley, a bathroom with showers, sleeping room for six people, and its own generator for air-conditioning and electricity. It was ideal for my family of six. I sold the twenty-eight-foot Reinell and made money on it and bought the bigger yacht for twenty-two thousand dollars. The rule of thumb in those days was that every foot of the boat was worth about one thousand dollars, so that boat should have cost me thirty-three thousand dollars. I fixed the boat a little bit, changed the drapes, and painted it. I added a canvas top to the flybridge. My friends had a ball with it. I took them deep-sea fishing out in the gulf several times. I took my family to Sarasota's intercoastal waters. We docked and slept in the boat just outside a big restaurant where we would have dinner.

I met the owner of the house that was built next door. His name was Max Weber, and he was a very enterprising young man from Colorado. We got to know each other, and he informed me that he had found two beach lots in Sunset Beach on Treasure Island. He was building a beachfront home on one lot and asked if I wanted the other lot. He showed me the lot and the house he was building. The zoning on the beach required the house to be built on stilts; the living space had to be one floor up with nothing below. He sold me the lot for fifty thousand dollars, and I paid him another seventy thousand for the three-bedroom stilt home. It took him several months to build the house because he was doing most of the work himself. When it was finished, it had a two-car garage with a screened-in bottom floor, a billiard table, and a ping-pong table. I parked my two antique cars in the garage. Now, I have two houses. We used the beach house for parties and the guesthouse for visitors. Boy, did we have a ball!

My practice was up and booming thanks to Dr. Norton. He had me named emergency room chief at the Lake Seminole Hospital, and I was elected chief of surgery and member of the board of governors of the hospital.

The Filipino-American Club of Pinellas County

I met a Filipino doctor who worked at the VA Hospital at Bay Pines, and he informed me that there were a lot of Filipinos in the community, which I had not been aware of. I got their names and telephone numbers and started talking to them about forming an organization. A Filipino old-timer who had been in Pinellas for quite some time helped me get in touch with the rest of the Filipinos. His name is Al Pulido, and he had many relatives in the area. Our first get-together was in VA Veterans Park. I met a lot of Filipinos, and we decided to form a club. It was our insatiable desire to coexist that culminated in the formation of the Fil-Am Club of Pinellas County. At first, there were merely a handful of Filipinos and Americans in the club. But it did not take too long before it caught on; and the club still exists today after thirty-four years.

On December 7, 1975, a dinner dance with induction of officers was held at the Sheraton Hotel in St. Pete Beach. I was the first president and founder. Our guest speaker was State Representative Dick Deeb. Old and young people alike performed native dances in authentic Filipino costumes. It was a nonpolitical society, organized for the purpose of teaching Filipino-American children born and reared in the United States to know Filipino traditions, beliefs, customs, and culture.

FILIPINO AMERICAN CLUB

St. Petersburg International Folk Fair Society (SPIFFS)

When I was in the process of organizing the Filipino-American Club in the last few months of 1975, I got a call from Bethia Caffery, a staff writer at the *St. Petersburg Independent News*, who said she was forming a coalition of various ethnic groups for the bicentennial celebration of the United States.

Her point man, who became the executive director, was John Mallou, a Frenchman. We had an organizational meeting and officially formed the St. Petersburg International Folk Fair Society (SPIFFS). I was one of the founding members of the thirteen original ethnic groups and was elected treasurer. In the early part of 1976 Bethia was able to get a group of two dozen or so ethnic groups to participate in the bicentennial celebration.

The SPIFFS celebrated the Bicentennial Folk Fair from February 20–22. It was held at Bayfront Center. Working with the St. Petersburg Bicentennial Committee, chaired by Pat Mason, the SPIFFS has coordinated the fair to be a three-day festival of costumes, song, dance, music, cultural displays, and food of ethnic groups from around the world. Each group has its own arts and crafts in a booth and folk dances on the stage. I requested the help of Miss Carmilita Galang, a former schoolteacher who was elected secretary of the Fil-Am, to help us form the children dance group with my kids in the group.

(She has since passed away. May her soul rest in peace.) The children's various dances included the famous bamboo dance, the tinikling.

In the following years of the SPIFFS celebration I needed a more sophisticated dance ensemble. I sought the help of Mr. Joey Omila, one former member of a dance group from the Philippines, which had toured the United States to show the art of Philippine folk dances. They were members of the Filipino Association of Tampa who had organized in 1978. Every performance was followed by standing ovation. He had become a traveling agent and still managed the Philippine folk dances every year in our new building in Oldsmar through the Philippines Cultural Foundation Incorporated (PCFI). This is still funded by grants from the state of Florida and all the proceeds from a yearly three-day celebration in early spring. It is the only standing building in the United States made by the hardworking Filipinos in the Tampa Bay area. This was the culmination of my goal, accomplished with the help of Bobby Ruelo, an attorney, as well as Bill and Claire Ick, an enterprising, brilliant, and hardworking married couple whom I was fortunate enough to know. I relocated my practice to Texas during the building process, which started in 1995. The PCFI has two areas of functions. The big building is rented for big occasions like wedding parties, birthdays, and conferences, so it is paying for itself. The other section is for food and crafts, and it has built-in booths and a center stage for performances by local performers as well as Filipino artists from our faraway homeland.

Those were fun and busy days. The officers and my family made several television appearances locally. On March 4, 1976, the officers of SPIFFS were each awarded keys to the city of St. Petersburg by Mayor Charles Schuh for our hard work and participation in the Bicentennial Celebration.

My surgical practice was doing very well. I was the first surgeon in the bay area to use surgical staples in surgery. The company sent me to the University of South Florida to learn how to use the stapling device in surgery in the late seventies. This was followed by the use of endoscopy, which was invented by the Japanese to look into the gastrointestinal tract. Nobody knew how to use it in its infancy. We didn't have a gastroenterologist at that time, so I spent two weeks in Boston's Lahey Clinic to be trained in how to perform colonoscopies. I brought my family with me, and we explored the Boston area and went to Cape Cod and to see Plymouth Rock.

I was the only one at that time who knew how to use the endoscope, and that helped my practice quite a bit. The barium and upper GI series X-rays were beginning to be used less and less.

St. Petersburg International Folk Fair Society

FOLK FAIR

Bayfront Center MARCH 11-13, 1977

S.P.I.F.F.S.

S.P.I.F.F.S.
PRESENTATION OF KEY TO THE CITY OF SI. PETERSBURG

The Philippine Medical Society of Florida

Around 1977 or 1978 a lot of Filipino doctors came to St. Pete and started to practice. They came mostly from up north, probably because they got tired of the weather. The weather in Florida is about the same as in the Philippines. I rounded them up, and we met at one of the conference rooms of a bank in St. Pete. A Filipino urologist kept interrupting me during the meeting. I did not know him or his ulterior motives at the time, and I found out later after that he had been the president of the Philippine Medical Society in the Philippines and had been the professor of a few doctors who were then practicing in St. Pete. During the election he became the first president, and I became the vice president. I did not say anything because all his students voted for him.

After the election, he kept calling me and asking me for advice. I thought he knew how to organize people and how to go about it, but the Philippines is very different from the United States. I told him that to be recognized as an association the organization had to be incorporated as a non-profit to avoid personal liability and also had to be registered in the state. I gave him my lawyer's name to see if he could help him.

We had set our objectives as the promotion of a higher level of professional competence, ethical conduct, mutual assistance in the establishment of medical practice and in safeguarding rights and privileges, promotion of goodwill and mutual cooperation among the medical and allied professions in Florida and neighboring states, and enhancement and active participation in continuing medical education.

In March of 1978 we had our induction ball at Feather Sound Club in Clearwater.

In 1979, I decided to move closer to my office in Seminole. I found a place to build a house, Lake Seminole Country Club. It took me about forty-five minutes to get to my office one way. It was also closer to the school my children attended, St. Petersburg Catholic School in the Tyrone area. During the process of building my third home, I sold my boat and made a profit (which is unheard of since usually people lose money when they sell boats). The trick was that you had to buy your boat cheap. I sold my two antique cars too to a guy from Ohio who saw the cars during an auto show. . He gave me his card and told me to call him if I decided to sell the two cars. I made a little profit.

While we were still in the Broadwater area, my classmate Celso Samaniego and his wife visited us. He was practicing anesthesia in Flint, Michigan. We talked about everything, from the past to the future. He told me that he was looking at a house in Daytona Beach, also a waterfront property like mine. I guess he was also doing all right but still did not like snow.

While the house in Lake Seminole Country Clue was being built, I sold the house in Broadwater and used the proceeds of that to pay for the lot in the country club. We moved into the beach house. All of our furniture was stored in the garage, and we lived there for at least six months until the house in Seminole was done. It was a two-story, five-bedroom house with an Olympic size pool with screen enclosure and a big lake behind it. We stayed in the house for twenty years. The kids basically grew up there and eventually left us to go to college. They never came back and were on their own after their college graduation.

We experienced the good and bad sides of living on the beach. The good side was hearing the waves of the ocean, which was calming, and on the weekends seeing young women with T-back bathing suits strolling on the beach. The bad side was the salt air coming into the house and rusting all the metal appliances we had. I had to change the air conditioning unit outside within five years, almost its half-life.

In the early eighties, the Northside Hospital in Pinellas Park was owned by Gateway Corporation. A friend of mine at the corporation advised me to buy a debenture bond on the hospital. I just paid interest on it without a collateral. A few years later, the hospital was sold to Humana Corporation and made a windfall profit. I distributed most of the profit equally to my children for their college educations. I missed some boats in business—but not that one!

In 1983 I took my family on a twenty-eight-day tour of Europe on a bus and ferries. We started on June 6, 1983, traveling from London to Dover and taking a ferry to Brussels, Belgium. We boarded a bus, and the odyssey began. In Amsterdam, drugs are legal. They were selling marijuana plants on the streets! You could see the young guys walking on the streets all doped-up! As we walked around, the people on the streets were looking at us strangely, and I wondered why. So I looked around and saw some women displayed in the windows. We were in the red light district of Amsterdam! I immediately took my family out of there and went in a different direction away from the area.

In Germany we went to Cologne and Frankenthal. We did

some shopping in Basel, Switzerland, visited Lake Lucerne and Innsbruck, and stayed overnight in Salzburg, near Vienna, Austria. Salzburg was where the movie *The Sound of Music* was filmed, and the kids liked it.

In the morning we headed for Venice, Italy. We went to St. Mark's Square and took a gondola ride in the afternoon. We had lunch there, and I cannot forget the spaghetti I ate. It had one big meatball with a sauce. I had tasted a lot of meatballs before, but this one topped them all! In the early morning hours we headed for Greece through Yugoslavia, which was still a communist-occupied territory. We had lunch in Belgrade, and the food we ate was just excellent. It was a combination of Spanish, French, and Italian cuisine. We reached Salonica in Greece and traveled through a mountainous path toward Delphi, which is famous in ancient history for the Oracle of Delphi. In Athens we stayed overnight for a few days. We all know that Greece is the cradle of Western civilization and that the Romans patterned their philosophy and architecture. We visited the Acropolis and Parthenon. There was a lot to see, including remnants of the old civilization. In Olympia, we saw where the first Olympics began and viewed various old sports fields.

From Petra we took a ferry to Brindisi, Italy, and rode the bus to Naples. We took a ferry ride to the Isle of Capri, the location of Emperor Augustine's summertime palace. It had a cavern with blue water that was so clear you could see the bottom. We stayed there overnight. We took the ferry back to Naples and headed for Rome. If you really want to see antiquities, this is the place to be. The coliseum, the Spanish steps, and the famous fountain where *Three Coins in the Fountain* was filmed. From Rome we went to the Leaning Tower of Pisa and then to Nice, France. You should have seen the eyes of the Americans on our tour bus when they saw a topless beach with people of all ages, from pediatric patients to the Medicare population. We passed by Lyon and headed toward Paris where we stayed for a few days. We had lunch at the Eiffel Tower and went all the way to the top. What a view of Paris! Hitler spared Paris during his occupation because of its beauty. The Notre Dame Cathedral was just magnificent. There was a replica of the Statue of Liberty located between the east and west bank of the river. And we saw the Arc de Triomphe and the resting place of Napoleon Bonaparte.

We took the bus again and headed for Brussels where we took a ferry and then boarded a bus heading back to London before going back to the States.

My youngest son Chad was about twelve years old, and the oldest, Christine, was in high school then. They were old enough that they would later be able to remember everything they had seen and learned about how people live in Europe. When we crossed a river or a mountain, we would discover a different culture, language, and currency (they didn't have Euros in those days) on the other side. I never told my children of my difficulties when I was growing up and in school; all I showed them was the life of an upper-middle-class family in the States. They would learn in the future that my wife and I had started with nothing. Zero!

My practice continued to improve despite my frequent absences. My secretary was a girl name Paula, and , did she know how to collect! I told myself I would have to pay for her retirement whenever she quit her job. I noticed that after her work, she did nothing. I hated to see a brilliant mind get wasted, so I suggested she take up nursing in her spare time. St. Petersburg Junior College had a two-year course for nursing after high school. Being a secretary, the most she could get was twelve dollars per hour. She took my advice and got some grants and a scholarship and became a nurse (RN). It took her about three years, but she did it.

I started publishing scientific articles from 1983 until 1987. I published four medical articles and reported them to the *Journal of the American Society of Abdominal Surgeons.* I got my board certification in 1986 and became a fellow of the American Board of Abdominal Surgery. I got a call from Dr. Cordon from Brandon to find out if I wanted to relocate my practice to Brandon. I was busy then, and I told him I could not do it. I think they needed a general surgeon in Brandon.

I had another windfall profit when I sold my beach house. Again, I put the profits away for my kids' college educations.

I had owned the beach house for seven years, and being at the ocean, it would have deteriorated rapidly if nobody was living in it.

In the summer of 1984, I took the family to Portugal, Spain, and France. We took our time and enjoyed the scenery. In Paris, we visited the Louvre and did some shopping in town. We went to Avignon, which was the original Papal seat of the Pope before Vatican.

We explored Spain—Barcelona, Valencia, Granada, Malaga, Madrid, and other places—where we saw our first bullfight with a matador. After killing the bull they dragged it in with three horses. Beside the arena, there was a restaurant that served the bull meat, but we passed on that. In Malaga we could see the Moors' influence. (Spain had been under the Moors' control for at least four hundred years.) Their influence showed in the architecture of the buildings and in the people of Malaga, who had dark curly hair, fair skin, and beautiful eyes. There was not much to see at the Rock of Gibraltar except that it was well-inhabited by monkeys. In the northern part of Spain the inhabitants had white skin, and some had blue eyes and blond hair. The priests of the Augustinian Order from this area were teaching at San Sebastian College. In Seville we attended a dinner show with flamenco dancers and paella.

Toledo was pretty and very medieval, with narrow,

cobblestoned streets. The town was enclosed with a wall surrounded by a canal.

The main attraction in Portugal was the site of the Apparitions of Fatima. In 1916 three little children from a small village in central Portugal saw an angel on three different occasions. The following year, the three children saw the Lady of Light above a small oak tree. The lady asked them to return on the thirteenth of the month for the next five months. From the second occasion onward the apparitions were witnessed by an ever-increasing number of people; this culminated with a startling spectacle of light in the sky on the sixth occasion. The story spread all over the world. We only spent two weeks on the vacation that time around and headed back to the States after sightseeing in London.

Back to work again, I used a lot of staples in surgery on bowel resections and skin sutures. Humana sent surgeons for continuing education on laparoscopic surgery, mainly cholecystectomies and laparoscopic appendectomies. I did quite a few of these but my gallbladder cases were severe and required old-fashioned open cholecystectomies.

On December of the same year we spent our Christmas in Mexico City and New Year's in Acapulco. We toured the city landmarks like the site of the fountain of Tenochtitlan, now called Mexico City. We also saw the site of the Aztec ruins, the holy temple known as La Villa de Guadalupe ,which was built during Spanish rule. We went to the Sun-Moon Pyramids at Teotihuacan, an ancient Aztec city that flourished two thousand years ago. The largest pyramid was 250 feet high.

The National Museum of Anthropology featured the treasures of the Aztecs and Mayans. This is where I learned that our Filipino male customs called barong Tagalog came from the Aztec Indians. The Manila-Acapulco trade during Spanish times lasted for several hundred years. Goods from the Orient and Manila were brought in by the friars and vice versa, and English buccaneers targeted these loaded Spanish galleons. We went to Plaza del Toro for a bullfight with the matador just like we had in Spain. At night we attended a folk dancing show called Ballet Folkorico de Mexico.

We spent our New Year's in Acapulco. We stayed at the Princess Hotel right on the bay. We spent some time on the beach drinking fresh coconut juice, and my son Chad got to experience parasailing. He went up and away toward the bay and landed back on the beach. The following day we had lunch at the Hotel El Mirador and watched the cliff divers. Again, the family went shopping. My son Charles was crazy about Ralph Lauren shirts at the time, so we went and look for the Ralph Lauren shop. Luckily there wasn't one. I got away that time.

In 1988 my wife felt a lump in her right breast during a self examination. I sent her to my friends in the X-ray department, and the test results showed possible malignancy. She had a family history of breast cancer; her older sister had discovered breast cancer during her pregnancy. She had refused to abort, and she died after giving birth a few months later.

I scheduled my wife for a breast biopsy with frozen section with a possible modified radical mastectomy (removal of the breast glands and removal of the lymph nodes in her underarm). The administrator of the hospital talked to me about doing the surgery myself. I told him, "I know all the surgeons in town, and I know I am the most qualified one. Thanks for your concern, but I'd rather do it myself." I even told him, "For your information I even delivered my first child in Saginaw." The surgical biopsy showed malignancy, and I did the surgery, taking the breast gland and leaving the muscles underneath and dissecting her underarm to take most of the lymph nodes. A few days later the results of the pathology report came in. Immunoassay laboratory examination indicated the tumor was estrogen-positive, which meant that removing or curtailing the estrogen in her body might cure the cancer. I sought the opinion of my oncologist friend, and he recommended she start on anti-estrogen medication and take it for the next five years. In those days the only anti-estrogen drug available was tamoxifen, a very expensive drug that I had to buy in Mexico on my short trips to Cancun. Luckily my sister Luzviminda in New York who is working in Jamaica Hospital knew somebody in the pharmacy who was able to supply me with the medication at a cost. She had three positive nodes in her underarm, which was an irrelevant amount.

In 1994 she felt another lump in her left breast. The radiologist friend talked to me regarding her mammogram results. They were not sure about the report because the lump was located in the tail end of the breast tissue going toward the armpit. I scheduled her for surgery. The frozen section was positive, and again I did a modified radical mastectomy and started her on Tamoxifen. There has been no recurrence up to this date 2010, and she is now seventy years old.

A few years later she got a call from the Philippines that her younger sister also had breast cancer of the breast. She underwent a successful surgery and is also still alive and well today. As I have mentioned before, my second child, Cheryl, who was a BSN and had a master's degree in nursing passed away at the age of thirty-eight. One year after the diagnosis was made, she developed a very malignant non-estrogen-responding tumor. She was given chemotherapy by Moffit Medical Center.

Because of this very strong family history, I advised my first-born, Christine, to have her DNA tested. She took my advice, and the test showed she was positive for malignancy. She had a bilateral prophylactic simple mastectomy done with Silastic implants.

In those days, it was very difficult to sell patients prophylactic mastectomies. In all the breast surgeries I did I tried to convince the patients of the need to remove the opposite breast. Neither the medical community nor the insurance companies were in tune with the idea. I told my patients to continue their self-examination and have mammograms every year instead of every three to five years as recommended by everybody in the medical community. Members of the medical community seemed to forget that the breast is one organ in two separate locations; if one is cancerous, you can expect the other one to be as well.

Philippine Medical Society West Coast Chapter
Florida

Historical Facts
Philippine Cultural Foundation, Inc.

The Making of the Bayanihan Arts Center....

The completion of the *Bayanihan* Arts Center in the Philippine Cultural Enrichment Complex in Tampa is the work of a seamless, integrated fabric of talents that blended perfectly and consisted of generous and focused people who diligently and unselfishly gave their time and energies starting in 1995 when the Philippine Cultural Foundation, Inc. was founded all the way to the grand opening day of the Arts Center on September 22, 2001.

At the time when Roberto Ruelo came to Florida from Chicago in the early 1990s, there were already efforts and talks about building a small cultural center primarily by members of the Pilipino-American Association of Tampa Bay (PAAT). In the late 1992, Cesar Domagas, then president of PAAT, appointed Bob Ruelo to chair its clubhouse committee. Finding that the lot donated by Dr. Bobby & Josie Villanueva to PAAT for its clubhouse was small and that PAAT alone cannot build a center for all the community to use, Bob decided to involve the various organizations in the community. This led to the formation on June 9, 1993 of the not-for-profit Philippine Cultural Center and Library Title Holding Corporation (THC). The incorporators were:

Bill Ick of the Philippine Performing Arts Company (PPAC), Rudy Curioso of the Pilipino-American Political Aggregation (PAPAG), Maria Feir of PAAT, Dr. Ben Abinales of the Philippine Medical Society of Florida West Coast Chapter (PMS), Dr. Carlos Soriano of the Filipino American Club of Pinellas County (FACPC), Ed Pabilonia of the Philippine Nurses Association of Tampa Bay (PNA), Ed Bilbao of Ang Bisaya of Florida (ABF), Bert Almeda of the Phil-American Kiwanis Club of Florida (Kiwanis), and Linda Capua of the Philippine Medical Auxiliary Florida West Coast Chapter (Auxiliary). The idea was for each organization to be the owner of the cultural center and library in proportion to its contribution in the construction of the building. Joey Omila was elected the first president of THC. Claire Ick who went along with her husband to attend meetings volunteered to help Dr. Ben Mosquera who was in charge of fundraising. As chairman, Claire introduced the concepts and named the first charity event the "Sampaguita Ball." Committee members Dolly Mosquera, Maria Raffinan, Clem Lazaro, Luz Pinder & Lari Cummings diligently worked that resulted in the most successful and well attended first reserved seating event in Tampa Bay. Joey Omila and Claire developed the Sampaguita Ball logo, Joey coming up with the dancing partners in terno and barong tagalog and Claire adding the Sampaguita lei around it. Henceforth, Sampaguita Ball concepts have been adopted at all formal events in Tampa Bay, including the cena de media noche (midnight snack) that has now become a staple of all formal parties in Tampa Bay. Sampaguita Ball '94 and '95 were both chaired by Claire. As another fundraiser program, Claire and Bill Ick initiated the handling of a concession stand for the Lightning Hockey Games at the Tropicana Field (then the Thunderdome) that earned the corporation its first $10,000. With those successes in her resume, Claire was asked by Bob to run as the next president of the Title Holding Corporation. Claire told Bob that the only way she will accept the presidency was if the corporation would become a nonprofit tax-exempt corporation that would be owned by the Filipino-American community, rather than the contributing organizations. She was convinced that if the community worked together to build their center the probability of success would be much higher. Her thought was that in order to achieve the goal of building a center and not continually assess the community, the corporation must establish annual events that would eventually partially support the Center when built and to spend all donations and fundraising income on the purchase of a piece of land and step by step build on the property that will entice the community to donate more as they see their money going to something that they can enjoy now and not later. Intrigued and finding that the incorporating organizations were not contributing as hoped for, Bob convinced the THC to be the incorporator of the Philippine Cultural Foundation, Inc.

(PCFI) which was incorporated on March 28, 1995, dissolve the THC, and transfer all of its assets to the PCFI. Claire was elected first president of PCFI.

On July 3, 1995, PCFI bought its first 5-acre property at Nine Eagles Drive with the funds generated from the Thunderdome concession project, large donations from PPAC and PAAT, proceeds from the Sampaguita Ball '94 and other fundraising events and grass roots contributions. The choice of the location of the property was dictated by the requests of the Filipino American community that it be centrally located between Hillsborough and Pinellas Counties. On July 19, 1995, Bob secured from the Internal Revenue Service the PCFI's Section 501©(3) organization tax exempt status. After closing on the property, Claire stunned the board of directors of PCFI by proposing to have the first Philippine Festival the next year, April 1996. Bill enjoined to convince the Board that the project was feasible and manageable. Reluctantly, the Board voted to go ahead with "PhilFest" (name was coined by Joey Omila from Philippine Festival and was subsequently registered service mark by Bob).

After the site planning and permitting work by Roger Caculitan, the Board and many volunteers headed by the Philippine Basketball Association then president Gerry Canezo, Butch Nivera, and Butch Lotuaco who donated the first sign that says "Future Philippine Cultural Center" on the property, started cutting trees and leveling the swampy

5-acres, together with members of the PAAT, PASL and others. Efforts to fundraise to pay for fill, contractors fees, etc. were abound…a tennis tournament chaired by Dr. Cesar Ruiz, bowling tournament sponsored by the Philippine American Sports League headed by Frank Estrada & Fred Llenarez, and the Phil-Am Bowling League members. There were also the Fun Kruz chaired by Joey Omila, bingo/majong/poker parties, dances, etc. On September 24, 1995, James Jamo chaired the ground breaking picnic at a small cleared area of the 5-acre property. Every one was jubilant. It was a day many would always remember.

Three weeks prior to the festival in April of 1996, some members of the board visited the site, they were shocked to find the grounds to be still muddy and filled with water. There were suggestions to cancel the event, despite the fact that ticket sales have been sold and billboard signs underwritten by Dr. Cesar Cruz to publicize the event were already up. Claire persisted. Initiated by Dr. Mike Dionaldo who first handed her his check, the Board gave Claire about $9,000 in donations to pay for fill and pay the contractors. The excitement and generosity of the community were astounding after that, with Aurora Fortson donating her design/architectural skills and who designed the first architectural concept of the Cultural Center that became PCFI's logo for the next five years, Roger Caculitan and Arnel Santos sharing their engineering skills, Dee Perez volunteering his time and equipment to help clear the property with the help of Roland Lazaro, Val Blanco, Rocky Barrido, and many others.

Confidently, Bill Ick chaired the first PhilFest on April 13 & 14, 1996, with committee members Bob Ruelo, Joey Omila, James Jamo, Roger Caculitan, Bing Curioso, Rudy Curioso, Jojo Lontok, Claire Ick, Frank Estrada and Roland Lazaro The group was then fondly referred to as the "dream team". Jojo brilliantly suggested the Miss PhilFest contest that was seconded by Joey Omila who was in charge of entertainment. On the first day of that memorable two-day weekend, the first group of food vendors, - Regina's Food Products, Jolens, Maxims, Aling Fely, Bob & Chris Shum, and Jimmy Jimenez Lechons were flustered because at 2:00 p.m. on the first day they have already served all the food that they were supposed to prepare and serve for the next day Sunday. The PhilFest site was packed and side street parking for more than a mile on both sides of Nine Eagles Drive was bumper to bumper. Everyone was nostalgic with the first "arco" constructed and donated by Dr. Ernie Colina and the small Bahay Kubo donated by Dr. Jun Cordon. The small, shaky, rented stage was busy with the Philippine Performing Arts Company dancers and the Philippine Choral Group singers entertaining the more than 6,000 people who came to the first outdoor Philippine festival in Tampa Bay. Joey Omila, Jojo Lontok, Bing Curioso, Aba Villagomeza, Connie Chanrasmi, & Olive Santiano were all sweats and smiles as they led the fabulous entertainment extravaganza. Then there was the Arnis exhibition by the students of Dr. Willie Matias. The Bad Habitz Band, led by Dr. Ric Galura with Dr. William Cua, and the Total Sound Band entertained on a wooden platform and hundreds danced to their music till midnight. The Karaoke booth of Dee Perez was full of hopeful talents. Bob, Jean Ruelo and Rudy Curioso feverishly worked in ticket/food coupon sales and accounting for the donations. Jean, Vadjie Corpuz, Nilda de la Cruz, Shirley Seepersad, and Lita Iyog over the years alternately handled the daunting task of accounting for the Miss/Mrs. PhilFest donations. And what is a Philippine Fiesta without a Miss PhilFest? It was an absolutely beautiful pageant and a beautiful winner. The first Miss PhilFest was Angie Raffinan, daughter of Drs. Jun & Maria Raffinan who chaired the Hospitality Booth. At the end of that weekend, the entire community was energized!

The dust had not yet settled when Claire asked the Board to approve the purchase of another 5-acre adjacent property for use as parking area for the next year's festival. But PCFI did not have any money since the $51,000 net profit generated by PhilFest '95 was used to pay for the contractors and the almost 3- 5 ft soil and white stone fill for the site. With outstanding resolve, the Board approved for PCFI to get a short term loan from NationsBank to pay for the adjacent 5 acre property, with the guarantee from the PhilFest '97 chairman, Bill Ick, that the event will generate more than $50,000 to cover the loan. On September 1996, Maria Raffinan chaired the Sampaguita Ball at the Hilton Inn in St. Petersburg. On October 31, 1996, PCFI bought the second 5-acre parcel of land that was adjacent to the first 5-acre parcel. Once more, the volunteers went to work and the construction and property development committee was formed with Roger Caculitan, Aurora Fortson, Ed Pulido, Roland Lazaro, Bill Ick, James Jamo, Arnel Santos, Bob Ruelo, Rudy Curioso, Joey Omila and Claire Ick. Ho Ho's at Dale Mabry became their official meeting place with Bill Ick, Bob Ruelo, Roland Lazaro and others alternating to pay for the meal The group started the PCFI trend of not charging the Foundation for any of their meeting meals and expenses. PhilFest '97, led by the same dream team of PhilFest '96 added new vendors as Delio and Ellen Mata and Merly & Virgie Panganiban. Ambassador Raul Rabe graced the event with his presence. With the donation of Roland & Clem Lazaro of a silk screen machine, the PPAC dancers headed by Dan Rojas and Jay del Rosario produced the flags of the various participating organizations: Philippine Performing Arts Company, Maharlika Society of Florida, Ang Bisaya of Florida, Filipino-American Club of Pinellas, Phil-Am Sports League, Bicol Florida Association, Philippine Association of Ladies of MacDill, Philippine Medical Society, Philippine Medical Auxiliary, Pilipino-American Association of Tampa Bay, Philippine Nurses Association, Philippine Basketball Association and Philippine

American Political Aggregation. Their flags proudly stood at the festival. Added to PhilFest '97 was the Bingo booth, headed by Clem Lazaro and Estela Gennantonio with a lot of assistance from Dave and Nenita Sweet. With the generous support of Miss PhilFest '97 candidates, especially the '97 winner, Michelle Dy, the beautiful and talented daughter of Dr. Rodolfo and Rose Dy, PhilFest ended up with a $59,500 net profit versus the goal of $52,000. Bill and his committee made good of his promise. Three days after the event, PCFI paid off its entire loan from NationsBank. In the year 1997, Roland & Clem Lazaro became the highest individual donor until the year 2000, PAAT the highest association donor until 2001 and Regina's Food Store the top PhilFest vendor. Lari Cummings chaired the Sampaguita Ball '97 held at the Clearwater Convention Center.

1998 would bring a lot of exciting things for PCFI. When guests came for PhilFest '98, they found themselves entering the newly fenced property through the beautiful concrete/steel gate with a sign "Philippine Cultural Center" and the beautiful bamboo arco crafted and donated by Ver Bautista and the Morong group. The excitement and generosity of the community exploded. The pride of those who made it happen (the fence volunteers: Ver Bautista, Roger Caculitan, and all the PASL members, Val Blanco (painting), Ross Hermano, Roy Covarrubias, James Jamo, Ed Taghap and many others (site preparation) ; Jun Balderama, Ed Pulido, Rocky Barrido, and Mike Lebrias, worked on the electrical systems for the grounds and booths; the steel gate partially donated by Dee Perez; landscaping partially donated by Robert Enriquez, and the expenses were donated by generous community members and member associations) which were overwhelming. The food for the volunteers were donated and prepared by Roland Lazaro with the alternating help of Cleo Tagle and the PASL wives. PhilFest '98 with Bill continuing to be the chairman under the leadership of Claire, generated a gross income of $140,000 and net profit of $70,000. Thanks to the hard work of many volunteers and the generosity of the supporters of the Miss PhilFest candidates. A gracious winner, Michele Pilapil, daughter of Drs. George & Martha Pilapil, became Miss PhilFest '98 and her escort was Jun Cabigas, son of Dr. Virgilio & Lucy Cabigas, both families from Lakeland. The Sampaguita Ball '98 held on September 19 at the Tampa Convention Center broke past records in attendance and net profit of $30,000. It was an exciting grand evening with Dr. Patsy Abinales as chairman. 1998 also marked the beginning of the fundraising efforts for the Sinagtala Theater with the goal to complete it by PhilFest '99.

1999 was a year of success and upheaval for PCFI and the community as a whole. The goal was to construct the Sinagtala Theater prior to PhilFest. Roger Caculitan, as project manager, and Claire worked hand in hand to get the best deal for the steel roof of the Theater. First they thought the purchase price of $29,000 for one roof was good, but after a diligent search by Claire for a better deal, they came up with a steel company that offered two steel roofs (for the Sinagtala Theater and the Barangay Pavilion) at the price of around $25,000, throwing in the steel roof for the Bicol Pavilion for only $5,000. Immediately, Roger and Claire closed the deal and the heavy steel roofs were delivered unassembled by Friday before the Festival week. The committee and vendors panicked as all booths cannot be set up as the steel roof lay on the PhilFest grounds. Claire called a construction company called Caladesi Construction Company and literally begged them to assemble and install the roofs in time for the Festival that weekend. Caladesi was very accommodating and sent their crew and worked overtime that weekend to finish the installation by Thursday. Friday, PhilFest '99 opened its doors. Indak Pambata, with Bing Curioso as director, debuted at PhilFest '99. Again, the community was overwhelmed by the beautiful Sinagtala Theater, the Barangay Pavilion, the Bicol Pavilion and the Palaruan (playround). Maharlika Society of Florida, under the leadership of Rhose McGowan initiated and funded the playground. PhilFest '99 generated a gross revenue of approximately $155,000 and a net profit of approximately $70,000. Miss PhilFest '99 was Anna Tioseco, the beautiful daughter of Bonnie and Tina Tioseco, and her handsome escort was Rodney Bautista, son of Rudy and Lucy Bautista who would eventually become very active directors of

PCFI. The enthusiasm at the festival was so intoxicating that Ed Pulido and Nenita Sweet decided to solicit donations for the construction of the Ilocano Pavilion. Roger and Dr. Philip Lewis joined the effort that evening. This campaign led to the formation of the Ilocano USA. In the meantime, a group, headed by Jun & Maria Raffinan and Ben Mosquera, started their campaign for Maria Raffinan to run for president at the upcoming election in May 1999. Because of the different directions to which Maria wanted to lead PCFI, with the staunch support of Bob Ruelo, Bill Ick, the Lazaros, the Caculitans, the Curiosos, PPAC headed by Joey Omila, half of the PASL (James Jamo, Frank Estrada, Emeng Germino, Ross Hermano, etc.) and majority of the board members, Claire decided to run again for election, despite the fact that she was ready to retire, and formed her own slate of supporters. It was a contentious election based on two different platforms on how to proceed with the construction of the Cultural Arts Center. Claire was reelected to her fifth year as president winning with a slate of the majority of the members of the immediate past Board of Directors and new members who would become vital to the later success of PCFI. Ang Bisaya of Florida, Maharlika of Florida, Fil-Am Club of Pinellas County, and the Philippine Medical Society decided not to an active participating member of PCFI. The Phil-Am Sports League split up, half supporting PCFI and half deciding to resign from active participation with the Foundation. This resulted in the formation of the Sports Club of Tampa Bay, with Roland Lazaro as president and Dr. Ben Abinales as chairman. The Club, better known as TABASCO, became a very active participating organization of PCFI. Sampaguita Ball '99 was successfully co-chaired by Clem Lazaro and Amy Estrada.

Working closely with Bob, Roger, Rudy and Emeng Germino, Claire diligently wrote a grant application for $500,000 from the State of Florida for the community arts center. To meet the requirements of the State, Bill and Claire solicited the help of their son, Mark, now a financial consultant for DeLoitte & Touche to perform, pro bono, a feasibility study on the capability of the Filipino community to support a cultural arts center and formulate a business plan which otherwise PCFI would not have been able to afford to pay for. Claire recommended to the Board that the entire 10-acre be called the Philippine Cultural Enrichment Complex, together with naming the different structures on the facility as Sinagtala Theater, Barangay Pavilion and Bayanihan Arts Center. On July 9, 1999, 19 copies of the application and feasibility study were sent to the State of Florida, Division of Cultural Affairs. Bob Ruelo, Claire Ick and Rudy Enrille burned thousands of hours talking, and writing to the legislature and arts council members to lobby for the grant. On November 3, a delegation consisting of Bill & Claire Ick, Bob & Jean Ruelo, Joey Omila, Roger & Angie

Caculitan, Rudy Curioso, Emeng Germino, Val Blanco, James Jamo, Rudy Enrille and Rev. Christian Villagomeza went to Jacksonville for the Florida Arts Council meeting to make PCFI's formal presentation of the grant. At this meeting, the Florida Arts Council approved the grant and a few weeks later, the Secretary of State, Katherine Harris, recommended PCFI's grant to the State Legislature for funding. American Express Company, through the efforts of Glenda Roepcke and Bob Wood, gave PCFI a $10,000 grant. In December, Ambassador Ernesto Maceda visited the Philippine Cultural Enrichment Complex and inaugurated the Ilocano Pavilion which was proudly built by its members. PASKO was born on December 18, 1999, conceived and chaired by Clem Lazaro and Amy Estrada.

The year 2000 was a dizzying year for PCFI, breaking its record in terms of numerous activities such as cultural , social and fundraising. PhilFest 2000, still chaired by Bill Ick, on April 7, 8, & 9, broke all-time records in terms of gross revenue of $214,000 , a net profit of $122,0000 and bolted out previous records in vendor participation and attendance. Fundraising parties for the Mrs. PhilFest candidates were in abundance prior to the Festival. There were Las Vegas nights, bingo and majong sessions, dances, spaghetti/or whatever dinners, Rizal movie premier, etc. The PhilFest Committee, again headed by Bill, worked like there was no tomorrow. The Arco Project, chaired by Drs. Ben & Patsy Abinales, Drs.

Romy & Vickie Tagala, and Drs. Len & Terry Bissonnette was another great surprise to the PhilFest attendees. The Ilocano USA proved their unity and fundraising skills by winning the Mrs. PhilFest , Bing Curioso, with escort Roger Caculitan. Old and new faces became familiar faces as they joined the PhilFest and other Committees, the Board and Advisory Board…Lito Dano, Raxtie Auza, Dr. Evelyn Gador, Dr. Philip & Merle Lewis, Drs. Romy & Vickie Tagala, Drs. Len & Terry Bissonnette, Dr. Judith Cimafranca, Dave & Nenita Sweet, Jun Balderama, Jimmy Abellada, Rudy & Lucy Bautista, Dr. Greto & Edna Ramos, Robert Enriquez, Mike Lebrias, Elena Garcesa, and Dr. William Cua, The Philippine Embassy, led by Ambassador Ernesto Maceda, introduced the very successful Consular-on-Wheels at PhilFest 2000. Bill Ick was elected president of PCFI in May for a two year term. American Express sponsored a very successful Hawaiian Luau Dance for the benefit of the PCFI; the Philippine Independence Day event was chaired by TABASCO, that featured the Hi-Pertensions, Rex Navarette and Paul Enriquez.; and the Florida Legislature appropriated the PCFI Grant of $500,000 in the 2000 Legislative budget. The Cultural Affairs Advisory Board was formed with Flossie Abrigo, Rey Aquino, Emma Cala, Connie Chanrasmi, Dr. Carlina Jimenea Launger, Beatriz Nunag, Dr. Rafael Pascual, Dr. George Pilapil, Edna Ramos, Dr. Gabriel Sanchez, Dr. Caridad Santos, Dr. Vickie Tagala, and Rev. Christian Villagomeza as its first group of members.

Dr. Vickie Tagala, Edna Ramos, Nenita Sweet, Loida Espiritu and Dr. Carol Lacson would later join this elite group.

On June 15, 2000, Florida's Secretary of State, Katherine Harris, wrote PCFI that the Foundation had been awarded the $500,000 grant under the Department of State's 2000-2001 Cultural Facilities Program. On August 20, 2000, the Division of Cultural Affairs received a letter from 18 members of the associations who decided not to support PCFI after the 1999. In the November 2000 issue of the official newsletter of PCFI, the Board of Directors sent an open letter to the community stating its position regarding the letter that was also published for the information of the community. On August 6, the Groundbreaking for the Bayanihan Arts Center, chaired by Jocy Omila, was held with a lot of fanfare, food and camaraderie. Plans for the construction of the Bayanihan Arts Center kept Claire Ick, Bob Ruelo , Roger Caculitan, Bill Ick, Rudy Curioso, Emeng Germino, Roland & Clem Lazaro, Ed Pulido, Jun Balderama and Jimmy Abellada busy who among themselves designed the building without the use of a an architect, thus saving this fee for PCFI. The Caladesi Construction Company as constructors and the R.C. Land Engineering Company as site engineers were awarded the contracts to build the Arts Center that was scheduled to start on January of 2001. Roger Caculitan was hired by PCFI as project manager and Bill Ick acted as the volunteer owner representative to oversee the project. Sampaguita Ball 2000 broke all previous records in attendance of 570 guests, gross income of $52,290 and a whopping $31,637 in profit. It was an outstanding achievement by Lucy Bautista, chairman. The Arts Council of Hillsborough County gave PCFI a grant of $20,000 for its cultural programs and American Express gave another $10,000. On December 16, 2000, PASKO, chaired by Clem Lazaro with the Sampaguita Committee, became another very successful event of the Foundation. Claire, the first and 5-year term PCFI president, was awarded the prestigious Philippine Presidential Award "Banaag" for the year 2000 for her outstanding achievement of leading the effort for the Filipino-American community to build the Philippine Cultural Enrichment Complex. Dr. Philip Lewis received the award for Claire from President Joseph Estrada in a ceremony in the Malacanang Palace in Manila.

On February 2001, the construction of the Bayanihan Arts Center commenced. The cultural classes of Iskwelahang Munti was a successful turnout. School principal, Rey Aquino, aka Tatang Miguel, and Ning Bonoan initiated the formation of the Heritage Enrichment Learning Program (HELP). Ning also established a Health Assistance Program with nurses and doctors in the Board and community. PhilFest 2001, 6th annual Philippine Festival, was chaired by Roger Caculitan who had met extra challenges in finding a parking area for the attendees of PhilFest due to the construction of the Bayanihan Arts Center on the 2nd 5-acre property. PhilFest

2001 broke past records for gross income and wall-to-wall attendance. Guests from all over the United States including Canada and Philippines bustled their way through the crowded PhiFest grounds. Janet Clark, a Filipino-American country singer was the guest artist at PhilFest. Ilocano USA once more showed their spirit of winning. Edna Ramos was crowned Mrs. PhilFest 2001 and her escort was Dr. Greto Ramos. The Independence Celebration for the 5th year was chaired by Frank & Amy Estrada. Joey Omila was officially offered the position of Executive Director to oversee the entire operation of the Philippine Cultural Enrichment Complex, including the Bayanihan Arts Center as a self-sustaining center and to establish cultural programs for the community. The marketing, publicity, budgets and interior design of the Arts Center were chaired by Claire Ick. As a result, Claire launched the underwriters program to help in furnishing the Arts Center. Immediately, Dr. Judith Cimafranca underwrote the Library and Drs. Len & Terry Bissonette underwrote a hall, followed by the Drapiza-Infante families, Dr. Maria Teresa Guerrero and Roland and Clem Lazaro. Rudy and Lucy Bautista underwote the huge 7 ft. crystal chandelier for the lobby and the underwriters donated the four capiz chandeliers for the Sampaguita Grand Hall. Lilibeth Lontoc expedited the purchase and donated shipping cost for the capiz chandeliers which was custom handcrafted specially for the Arts Center.

PCFI and the community finally has a Grand Opening of the Bayanihan Arts & Events Center to complete the Philippine Cultural Enrichment Complex on September 22, 2001, and held an Open House on September 23, 2001 chaired by Lucy Bautista, and the Sampaguita Ball 2001 on October 13th, chaired by Olive Santiano.

The evolution of where PCFI stands now is a testament to the hard work and dedication of a lot people. The success of PCFI is primarily attributed to those whose support never ceased for a moment since they became active in PCFI, majority of whom have joined since 1995 and are now permanent members of the Board of Directors. They are the parts that made the PCFI engine working continuously for the last six years. Claire Ick, under constant challenge to make it happen did not waver in her dedication to forge ahead with the project. Bill Ick and Bob Ruelo kept her going and who worked with her daily, 365 days a year, through 5 years of successes, heartaches and challenges. Their work for PCFI were constant, unwavering, 24-hours a day, 40 hours a week, 365 days a year and nonstop. In addition, they received no compensation of any kind from the Foundation despite the use of their combined professional skills in organization, management, legal and operations to lead the corporation from 1995 through the current presidential tenure of Bill. Additionally, five to six year PCFI veterans Joey Omila, Roger Caculitan, Angie Caculitan, Jojo Lontok, James Jamo, Lari

Cummings, Bing Curioso, Rudy Curioso, Val Blanco, Jun Balderama, Ed Pulido, Frank Estrada, Amy Estrada, Roland Lazaro, Clem Lazaro, Roy Covarrubias, Sylvia de la Cruz, Olive Santiano, Bing Santiano, Ross Hermano, Emeng Germino, and Ben Abinales ran the engine throughout the year. Other board members who joined to help pump the engine when it stalled were Mike Lebrias, Patsy Abinales, Dave Sweet, Nenita Sweet, Greto Ramos, Edna Ramos, Lucy Bautista, Rudy Bautista, Vickie Tagala, Romy Tagala, Len Bissonnette, Terry Bissonette, Philip Lewis, Merly Lewis, Judy Cimafranca, Jimmy Abellada, Aba Villagomeza, William Cua, Connie Chanrasmi, Esther Gianan, Robert Enriquez, Liberty Galloway, Evelyn Gador, Joe Baruta, Raxtie Auza, and Lito Dano. They are there when needed and will be part of this great endeavor for many years. The participating organizations whose continuous support of the Foundation kept the spirits of the leaders of PCFI from crumbling are the Philippine Nurses Association, Philippine Performing Arts Company, Pilipino-American Association of Tampa Bay, Ilocano USA, Ang Kaliwat Bol-anon sa Florida, TABASCO, Philippine Association of Ladies of MacDill, Bicol Association of South Florida, Philippine Choral Group, Filipino International Christian Church, Association of Filipino Students, and the Philippine American Political Aggregation, Inc.. There were countless volunteers to which PCFI owes its success, but the individuals mentioned who worked with 100% loyalty and dedication to PCFI and whose support have not wavered up to this celebratory moments are the heroes that made it happen and the threads that produced PCFI's seamless fabric of success.

Acknowledgement
Sponsors and Donors

The Sampaguita Ball 2010 Committee Gratefully acknowledges your Generosity

INVITATIONS
Liberty Galloway
Vivian Dudgeon
Lari Cummings
Carolina Lugay-Lacson, M.D.

VALET PARKING
Terry Bissonnette, M.D.
Len Bissonnette, M.D.

DECORATIONS
Arlene Floral Design

BAND/MUSIC/ENTERTAINMENT
David and Nenita Sweet
Evelyn Duterte Bondoc, M.D.
Rene Bondoc, M.D.
CapTrust Financial Company
Mary Ann Branesky
Edna Ramos
Angie Caculitan
Dr. Dom and Amy Uy

VIP ACCOMMODATIONS
Rudy and Lucy Bautista
Marly and Ross Balderama, M.D.
Romeo and Evelyn Gador, M.D.
Rocky and Emma Barrido
Tom and Imelda Evans
Letty Lancaster
Judith Cimafranca

MERIENDA-CENA
Clem Lazaro
Betty Covarrubias
Julie Germino
Anita Gonong
Mary Ann Branesky
Victoria Fabreo
Patsy Abinales
Manny Domisiw
Becky Jamo

PERFORMERS/USHERS ACCOMODATION
Roland and Clem Lazaro
Regina's Catering

To the Sponsors and Donors whose names have been inadvertently omitted, we apologize.
Your donations are greatly appreciated.

PHILIPPINE CULTURAL FOUNDATION, INC.
BOARD OF DIRECTORS, 2010-2012

Front Row (Left to Right):
Joey Omila, Aurora Curioso, Emeng Germino, Evelyn Gador, Jun Reyes, Edna Ramos, Roy Covarrubias,
Angie Caculitan, Roger Caculitan, Lucy Bautista, Rudy Bautista, Terry Bissonnette, Len Bissonnette,
Olive Santiano, Bing Santiano, Carolina Lugay-Lacson, Emma Barrido, Roque Barrido

Second Row:
Mary Ann Branesky, Julie Germino, Amy Estrada, Jojo Lontok, Marly Balderama, Betty Covarrubias,
Pacita Abinales, Vivian Dudgeon, Esther Giaman, Sylvia de la Cruz, Nenita Sweet, Clem Lazaro,
Merle Lewis, Helen Piloneo, Isabelita Smith

Third Row:
Arnie Paman, Greto Ramos, Ross Balderama, William Cua, Ben Abinales, Manuel Domisiw,
Carlos Soriano, David Sweet, Roland Lazaro, Philip Lewis, Arnell Biglete

Not in Photo:
Bert Almeda, Arturo Auza, Melissa Barrido, Joe Baruta, Val Blanco, Renato Boac, Frank Butron,
Judith Cimafranca, Lari Cummings, Rudy Curioso, Lito Dano, Evelyn Duterte-Bondoc, Rie Doquiles,
Rosemarie Dy, Robert Enriquez, Frank Estrada, Victoria Fabreo, Aurora Fortson, Liberty Galloway,
Romeo Gador, Ross Hermano, Bill Ick, Claire Ick, James Jano, Jess Loquias, Erlinda Pascual,
Rafael Pascual, Jean Ruelo, Roberto Ruelo, Melissa Santiano Martinez, Emy Santos,
Amada Sarnate-Bouffard, Vicky Tagala, Rose Tena, Christian Villagomeza

SAMPAGUITA BALL
2010
THE PHILIPPINES CULTURAL FOUNDATION, INC.
TAMPA FLORIDA

Malpractice

I had two malpractices cases brought against me in those days. One came in 1975 after I performed a vagotomy and pyloroplasty. In those days that was how we treated peptic ulcer disease; nowadays we treat it medically with a combination of two antibiotics and antacid medications. Peptic ulcers are caused by a bacterium called H. Pylori. The surgical procedure entailed cutting of the vagus nerve to the stomach (vagotomy) and then widening the opening of the end of the stomach, which is called the pylorus (pyloroplasty). After the surgery

I left for San Francisco to visit my brother-in-law. My wife had not seen her brother since we had left the Philippines. I asked another surgeon to cover for me while I was gone. On my return, the patient was still in the hospital. I spoke to the surgeon covering for me, and he told he that the patient was spiking a temperature. He opened the patient up and found a sponge inside the abdomen.

Before we close the abdomen in a surgery, the surgeon routinely asks for a sponge count. The sponge count was correct, so I closed the abdomen. I pulled the chart and double-checked the sponge count. The nurse had written down that the count was correct. I went to see the patient and showed him the chart note about the count. Abdominal X-rays were repeatedly done, and the radiologist had missed the sponge, which had a radio opaque lead metal in it so it could be seen in X-rays. When a surgeon performed a vagotomy and pyloroplasty, he or she would usually leave a sponge on the spleenic area to protect it from injury. This was the sponge I had left behind. I suggested to the patient that he see his lawyer. He filed a malpractice suit against the hospital, the radiologist, and me, since I was the captain of the ship. My insurance paid him a very negligible amount; the bulk of the payment came from the hospital and the radiologist.

My second lawsuit took place ten years later when a middle-aged woman came to my office with a lump behind her left knee, a Baker's cyst of the knee joint, which is similar to a ganglion of the wrist. The joint had to be immobilized for about a week. The patient was using crutches because of an underdeveloped right lower extremity; she had probably contracted polio when she was a kid. I assumed that she had probably been seen by another surgeon since the cyst was on the dominant leg, which would normally have been immobilized with a cast. That was my mistake; I did not immobilize the knee joint. My insurance settled the case without my permission. A few years later when I was working in the ER, she came in with some other complaint. I immediately recognized her and checked the knee; it was fine. Her friends recognized me and immediately left the ER.

Health Maintenance Organization (HMO)

In the late eighties the HMO (health maintenance organization), mainly for Medicare patients, came to town. Now, we doctors had a businessman between us and the patients. They were the ones who decided where the patients would go, and they had their own doctor referral system. We physicians knew nothing about HMOs. My friend (an internal medicine and pulmonary specialist) and I decided to join together and learn about HMOs by taking part.

The idea of the HMO is for the government to save money. They allocate a certain amount of money for each patient, and the providers (doctors) provide services including surgery and drugs. If you got patients who were in fairly good health, you had it made. If you got the chronically sick ones, you were out of luck. To start, Humana Corporation gave us five thousand patients. We rented a five-hundred-square-foot office across the street from St. Petersburg General Hospital and started our HMO in 1990. We hired two physicians and some paramedical staff to work in the clinic. We had a room converted for X-rays, and I opened an endoscopy suite with a recovery room that could accommodate four patients. Every Tuesday and Thursday I performed upper and lower endoscopies, morning and afternoon. They were all part of routine check-ups and treatment, if needed. My partner handled the medical part of the HMO, and I handled the surgical part, performing surgery if a patient needed it.

Being physicians schooled in the Philippines, we observed high ethics in our medical practice. We never denied patients their right to be treated the proper way, and we never gave them the run-around like other HMOs. The bad part of it was that you could not take care of patients properly on a set budget. In order for us to save more, we opened a pharmacy right in the office where the patients could get their medications on the spot. We were able to save some money that way. This went on for five years, and we had our ups and downs dealing with Humana Corporation. Later on we continued to have budget problems. Humana sent an administrator to work with us to handle the office personnel, and that took some of the load off our hands. Our office was streamlined to a bare minimum with some firing of personnel, and this worked for a while. Finally, Humana Corporation decided to change the picture. They hired another physician from India to take over. That was not a problem for us because we had just about had it. We had a smooth transition period while the new doctor learned how the clinic functioned. I continued performing endoscopies to the very end.

During my HMO escapade, I continued with my practice but was barely seeing patients. The referrals from Dr. Norton stopped. There was a good reason for this, and I felt like a traitor. He and another internist decided to form a corporation and built an office building with the assumption that I would be a tenant in their building. During the process of building, politics began, and I was the target. The other medical practitioners tried to convince me not to join the group— probably out of jealousy. That pressure kept mounting up and they reassured me that they would send me patients, but in the end they seldom did. I decided not to join the group, and through my mistake I learned a lesson: never bite the hand that feeds you.

In the late nineties I decided to close the office and went back to my old habits of working in ERs, locum tenens (temporary work while the surgeon is out of town), and as a jail physician. I traveled all over Florida and Georgia. I worked a week at a time and then went back home. As locum tenens I worked two to four weeks in small communities with full surgical privileges. I thought there might be a chance that they would need another surgeon, but those were false hopes. Communities were tight and unlikely to hire somebody from the outside.

During my practice in the seventies, eighties, and nineties, I experienced the golden years of Medicare. Medicare started in 1965, the year I came to Michigan. I can vividly remember when a surgeon scheduled a case in Saginaw General Hospital for an exploratory laparotomy (exploration of the abdominal cavity); I was the first assistant. He opened up the abdominal cavity, and the abdomen was filled with ascitic fluid. Further exploration revealed metastatic nodules involving the surface of the small bowel, and it was evident that the patient had widespread cancer producing the ascitis. The patient was an elderly female.

I asked him "What are we doing here?" (why are we operating?)

He replied, "Quiet."

At that time I was not aware of Medicare reimbursement and billing. A few years later while in practice I concluded that had been an abuse of Medicare benefits. My ethics were pretty high, since I had been educated in a Catholic university. I remember when physicians practicing in Florida had to take an ethics course as part of their continuing education for license renewal. To me that was just superfluous.

I continued moonlighting and just about exhausted my resources in Florida and Georgia. I had a friend in Georgia who informed me that there might be an opening in his place close to Tifton, Georgia, so I went to check it out. The place was a small town, but they did have a hospital. The town was too small for me though, and there was no entertainment around. I just did not like the place. I had kept my license in Texas active for several years and decided I would use it.

Twenty Outstanding Filipino Americans in the USA and Canada

In May of 1998, I got a call from my friend Dr. Ben Ocampo, a psychiatrist from Kissimmee, Florida, who said that I had been chosen as one of the twenty outstanding Filipinos in the United States. My friend had recommended me, and the honor was to be awarded in Manila. This was in conjunction with the Inauguration of the new Philippine president, Joseph Estrada. The swearing-in ceremony would be in Luneta Park right in front of Manila Hotel, where General MacArthur had stayed after liberation of the Philippines.

I have not been home for quite a while, and I was able to visit our neighborhood in Legarda. The building was still there, but it was abandoned and probably condemned. I visited my friend who owned St. Mary's School Supply. He was the one who had helped me by supplying the papers, stencils, and ink for my mimeographing machine.

We had meetings in Manila Hotel every day followed by a dinner. The topics were related to how we could help our native land with the expertise we had acquired in the United States. The recipients of the awards came from different walks of life, including a physician, engineers, pilots, and a common man who had made it good in the United States. One man in our group was retired from the Navy and had made money in real estate in Arizona during its developmental stage.

We met with senators, congressmen, government officials, and movie stars on a daily basis. One of the ladies who worked in the government complimented me, saying that I looked like a governor because of my features: I was tall and big and looked distinguished. I thanked her for the compliment. And she was right. During the swearing-in ceremony of the president, I went right in front of the podium and took pictures of him. Not one security person tried to stop me. I just walked in and out without anybody checking or questioning me. I think I gave the impression that I was somebody they dare not question.

We had a great time in Manila, and on our way home we went to Hong Kong as part of the itinerary. Dr. Ben Ocampo visited his relatives and we went on a tour later. I had been in Hong Kong several times before. We saw the new Hong Kong airport, which had just opened. It had been a British Colony and was a part of China by then. Even if Chinese citizens needed visas to enter Hong Kong.

Soon after my return from the Philippines I saw a Northwest Airlines advertisement for a five-day trip to Beijing for one thousand dollars for each of us, including airfare, food, and lodging. My wife and I booked the trip.

We departed on July of 1998 for Beijing, China. We stayed at the Jinglun Hotel right at the center of the city close to the American Embassy. I was expecting to find narrow streets just like in Europe, but to my surprise the inner-city roads were six lanes. There were a lot of bicycles and few private cars. There were three types of taxis available on the road. The best ones were for the well-to-do: yellow and air-conditioned. Going toward the American embassy, which was around the corner from our hotel, the streets were lined with vendors selling fake Louis Vuitton bags and Ty Beanie Baby dolls, as well as other knock-offs of well-known brands. You could not tell the difference between the fakes and the real ones. They were very good quality.

We went inside a big department store to do some shopping, and the prices of the goods were very cheap. Our tour bus took us to Tiananmen Square—what a sight! It was more than five acres of open area right in front of the Forbidden City, where the emperors lived for several hundred years, a city within a city. High walls with humongous gates surrounded the city. It was self-contained, intended to function alone. Inside the

Imperial Palace was the throne and the sleeping quarters for the concubines. The next stop was the Temple of Heaven, a huge tower arranged to sit in a big area with well-manicured lawns, just like our Washington Monument in D.C. Epcot at Disney World has a replica of the building.

The best attraction of them all was the Great Wall of China. It really is great! We could see the Great Wall rolling up and down the hills and mountains like a snake. It was built by workers using their bare hands; they used limestone blocks held together with a substance made of rice powder, an organic compound that has lasted lifetimes. The length of the wall is about three thousand miles, the distance from New York to California. I believe it was begun during the first Chin Dynasty and continued by the rest of dynasties that ruled China for many years.

When I visited Europe I thought it was great, but nothing can top China. History is being rewritten because of the new discoveries made in China when it opened its gates to the West. We all know about Marco Polo's trip and the introduction of noodles in Europe. We know about gunpowder. But most don't know about the cruise missiles the Chinese invented using bamboos, precursors of the rocket launchers used nowadays by the military. They were also responsible for the first compass for navigation, the first printing press, and the cannon (made using bamboo, of course).

We did not join the other tours because I had a map of

Beijing. I figured we could explore the city by ourselves. I asked the front desk to write "Beijing Zoo" and the "Summer Palace of the Emperor" in Chinese on the back of a hotel business card. I used the card to communicate with a Chinese taxi driver to take us where we wanted to go. We first went to the Beijing Zoo to see the pandas. The animals were big and beautiful, and they ate mostly bamboo pulp.

After that we went to the summer palace of Emperor Qianlong (1736–1795) of the Qing Dynasty. It was a tradition to set up bazaars (called palace bazaars) in the imperial palaces or gardens during religious festivals. They were waterfront shops. These masterpieces of Chinese landscape gardening were magnificent places to visit!

In our spare time we went shopping. We found a building five stories high that sold only cultured pearls, including black pearls. We bought a set of earrings, bracelets, and a necklace that was assembled in front of us with fourteen-carat gold plating.

We met some Filipinos who told us that the Holiday Inn near the airport was being run by Filipinos, from the manager to the cooks. We went and celebrated our Philippine Independence day there. We met the Philippine Ambassador to China, and of course they served Filipino foods including roasted pig (lechon). I asked one of the workers how they were getting paid and was told they were paid in U.S. dollars! I said, "What a deal!"

You will see Filipinos all over the world, especially on cruise ships. You know why? Because most Filipinos speak English. Our greatest export is human laborers who send their earnings home to their families, just like I did when I came to the States.

In September of the same year Northwest Airlines offered a similar deal for trips to Bangkok, Thailand. I had a friend from St. Pete, a general surgeon, who used to practice in St. Pete but had gone back home because his father was aging and he wanted his son to come back home. We stayed in the Dusit Thani Hotel in Bangkok right in the middle of the business district. This was my first time in Bangkok. I immediately noticed the similarity between Thai and Filipino people. It looked like I was in Manila. I theorized that Filipinos probably came from this part of southeast Asia, which consists of multiple islands, from Indonesia (including Sumatra) and Borneo all the way up to the Philippines. You could easily sail from one island to the next, but you would have to stop in the Philippines because after that is the Pacific Ocean.

Although the Philippine language is 60 percent Spanish, it is also similar to the languages of Indonesia and Malaysia. Most of the fruits we have in the Philippines they also have in Bangkok. We went to Wat Pho, the reclining Buddha and the Bangkok Grand Palace, a typical example of Buddhist architecture. It was magnificent! It looked like it was gold plated. Next we went to the temple of the Emerald Buddha, which was lined with mosaic emeralds. At night they took us to a show with pretty little women performing Buddhist folk dances. They could make a man wish he was a Muslim with plenty of wives.

Our next tour was by a trip by boat to the famous floating market of Thailand. It was unique and colorful, and all buying and selling of goods including snacks was done by boats. Most of what was for sale was fruits and vegetables and seafood. It was just fun to watch people trading on the small boats.

The Thai Village Cultural show was just great. There were folk dances, sword fights, and believe it or not, a bamboo dance similar to the ones we had in the Philippines, which again gave me the idea that Filipinos came from this part of the world. The main show was the Thai boxing, a mixture of boxing and kicking.

My wife had a ball riding the elephant—but did not like the smell! We saw elephants roaming the countryside all over Thailand.

I called my friend, the surgeon who had moved back to Bangkok from St. Pete and we met in the hotel lobby with his new Thai wife. He had been married before while he was in St. Petersburg and had three children. He divorced his American wife way before he left for Thailand. We had a good conversation, and his wife spoke English pretty well from being a stewardess in an airline. They had one boy though he questioned why he would have another child at his age. I told him that whatever will be, will be; you cannot control your destiny.

The hotel we were staying in was pretty nice. The garden in the swimming pool area was excellent and had a built-in waterfall. The hotel was in a commercial area, and we walked around and saw some shops. There were a lot of street vendors on the sidewalk, and a nearby alley was full of bars and strip joints. There were tailors and dress shops were all over, and they all sewed made-to-order items that could be picked up the following day.

The open market there was huge, with a lot of fruits and vegetables similar to what is found in the Philippines. The fast food street vendors were all over, and you could buy whatever your heart desires there. You should have seen the variety of seafood they had. We did not eat the exotic options, just the foods we were familiar with. We have a good time over there, just the two of us without any kids. I guess it was our second honeymoon. After five days we flew back to the States.

In the mid-eighties I got a call from my baby sister Inicita in the Philippines. She informed me that her husband had died during his visit to see their children. She and her husband were working abroad in Germany. He had died of complications from a severe asthma attack. He left her with five small children.

My sister had come to New York with my parents in the early seventies, and they had green cards. My parents left

New York after five years, but she stayed behind and then left for the Philippines a few years later, where she married her classmate from nursing school. They had five children and left them with their relatives in the Philipines while they worked abroad. He had made frequent visits to see the kids, but on that last visit he had a severe asthma attack and had died as a result of complications.

I told her to look for a house in Meycauayan Bulacan where my uncle Manolo lived; I would pay for it. They got a brand new house in a new development. After settling, she went back to work in Germany. She, her children, and her grandchildren are all here in the States now, living in Jacksonville, Florida.

1998 TWENTY OUTSTANDING FILIPINO AMERICANS IN THE U.S.A & CANADA

TWENTY OUTSTANDING FILIPINO-AMERICANS
IN U.S.A. & CANADA

28 DAYS EUROPEAN TOUR

CHAPTER 11

Texas

Pearsall

The following year, 1999, I got in touch with a recruiting company to help me find an emergency room job anywhere in Texas. The company informed me that there was one full-time opening in Pearsall, Texas, a small town south of San Antonio. I flew to San Antonio and visited the Riverwalk. It had changed a lot since my last visit in 1978 with my motor home. There is a shopping mall adjacent to the Riverwalk, and visitors can take boat rides as well. The river was lined on both sides with restaurant and shops. The following day I started driving south heading for Pearsall, about an hour's drive. It was a small town with a small twenty-five-bed hospital named Frio Hospital. I met the administrator of the hospital Mr. Holmes and the rest of the staff. They had a general practitioner who did OBs, C-sections, and pediatric practice, working with an OB-GYN doctor. There was also a general surgeon who did general practice, but no surgery.

Mr. Holmes showed me the town and the new hospital that was being built and said that they might need a surgeon in that new hospital. In the meantime I would working in the ER and wait. That suited me fine. I flew back home, picked up my stuff, and drove back to Texas. I stayed in a furnished one-bedroom with a kitchen that they provided me in a building that otherwise held the offices for the Home Health Care Services. I stayed there for a few months until I found a furnished three-bedroom house to rent.

On October 1, 1999, I opened an office near the hospital at Berry Ranch Road. I shared the office with a pediatrician. We had a ribbon-cutting ceremony, and all the medical staff, hospital staff, and dignitaries of the town were invited.

The *Frio-Nueces Current*, a local newspaper, published a story about the first gall removal performed by laparoscopy in town. Patients who needed that surgery were usually sent to San Antonio.

On December 16, 1999, I did Pearsall's first large bowel resection. The patient was an eighty-eight-year-old woman with a cancerous tumor of the large bowel. I resected the tumor and put the bowel back together with staples, just like old times at Lake Seminole Hospital. The *Frio-Nueces Current* published a story about that surgery too.

One day when the GP who delivered the babies was out of

town, a pregnant mother, who was passing through Pearsall with her family, went into labor and went to the ER. They were on their way back home to Houston, coming from Mexico. Guess who delivered the baby? Yours truly. The *Frio-Nueces Current* heard about it, and they took our pictures with the mother holding the baby. That was New Year's of 2000.

I had a chance to use my hand surgery expertise when a local cowboy walked into the ER with an injury to his right thumb. Apparently he had been lassoing a horse when his thumb got caught in a loop of rope. The horse had tried to get away from him and in doing do pulled off his leather gloves along with the full thickness of skin. You could see the tendons, bones, and other structures without the skin covering them. I explained to him that I was a hand surgeon from Florida and told him the exact procedure that should be done. He had the option of going to San Antonio. I explained to him that I was going to make or reconstruct a tube from the skin of his chest wall, insert the denuded thumb inside the tube, and suture it together. I would detached it from his chest wall after three weeks. He agreed to that, and I scheduled him for surgery. In the third week, I detached the tube from his chest wall. The post-operative follow-up showed that the skin was viable, that is, alive on its own.

I saw him several times after surgery to check on the viability of the graft. The skin was growing some hair, and he had to shave it every now and then because he had a chest full of hair. The skin graft that I placed on his chest, which I took from his right thigh, was also viable, and it healed well.

During the hospital staff meeting, I presented the patient before everybody in the room, and they were astonished at the results.

I explained to the patient that he should be careful handling hot items because he wouldn't be able to feel the heat. I also mentioned the island pedicle graft, which would give him sensation in his thumb, but he declined the surgery.

My other interesting case was misdiagnosed appendicitis in a ten-year-old kid. He had been having pains for months in his lower abdomen. When I examined him, I knew right away that he was suffering from chronic appendicitis that was misdiagnosed. I told the parents what I thought was the problem and that he would need exploratory surgery. They agreed. During surgery, I found a ruptured, chronically inflamed appendix with adhesions to the surrounding structures, including the small bowel. I resected the whole thing en masse (the whole inflamed part) and hooked the small bowel up to the large bowel. He did well after surgery.

Christine, my oldest daughter, paid me a visit from Atlanta with her husband. She wanted him to see San Antonio and the Riverwalk. I took them for a boat ride, and we ate in a Mexican restaurant. Christine could still remember the place, and it was definitely different from the last time she was there in 1978. I took them to the famous Alamo too.

Another interesting incident occurred when the GYN doctor was operating on a patient and trying to look for the ureter. When I walked into the room, he told me that he couldn't find the ureter. I told him, "I think that you are holding it in your hands." I told the nurse anesthetist to give him a five cc syringe with a 22-gauge needle. "Go ahead and aspirate the structure you are holding in your hand," I said. He did it, and urine came out. He was trying to anastomose the ureter to the urinary bladder.

I continued to work in the ER while operating occasionally. Being a small town, Pearsall would not support a general surgeon. The administrator and I had a conference, and he agreed to give me an extra five-figure salary monthly as soon as possible before we moved to the new hospital. The hospital opened in late 2001. I was at home in Florida on September 11, 2001, during the attack on the Twin Towers in New York. My son called me in the morning to tell me to turn the TV to any channel, and I saw the horror of the plane hitting the towers. That was devastating. The rest of the scenario you already know.

We moved into the new hospital, the Frio Regional Medical Center. It was right beside the highway. They built a helicopter pad within the compound because we are expecting traumas from vehicular accidents. Being the chief of surgery and the emergency room, I had to plan, and I performed my duties.

I found that in Texas there were a lot of diabetics with

kidney complication and microcirculation of the legs. Amputation and kidney failures were common occurrences.

I moved my office to the new building beside the new hospital. I leased office space with the GP who delivered babies and did C-sections. I delivered babies when he was out of town and occasionally did C-sections too.

On weekends if I was off work, I would usually go to San Antonio and entertain myself by going to the movies and shopping.

While working in the ER, I saw a male patient who was about twelve years old and complaining of pain in his testicles. I examined him and made a diagnosis of epididymitis (which affects the parts of the testicle consisting of ducts and vessels for the discharge of sperm). I gave him something for the pain and referred him back to the private physician who was a surgeon but was doing only general practice. What I heard was that he was seen by a nurse practitioner not his doctor and the kid had torsion of the testicle. I was never very clear about exactly what happened. The doctor never did talk to me. I believe he was talking to everybody and to the administrator, and they decided without my input that I would leave. In other words, it was purely political. I had had a gut feeling that that would happen. I just asked the administrator to give me time to look for a place, which he did.

The word spread around that I am leaving. On August 16, 2001, the *Frio-Nueces Current* published a letter to the editor entitled "Hard to Replace." It was written by one of my patients. Here is the letter from the newspaper verbatim:

Dear Editor,

Today in life, we are faced with many medical miracles one of them is Dr. Carlos Soriano.

Yes, A miracle, because he saved my life. I suffered from a medical condition for 32 years and never had the courage to undergo a surgical procedure. After hearing all the compliments about Dr. Soriano, I found the courage to visit his office. After having a brief moment with him, I was confident that Dr. Soriano was the best doctor to take care of me. My family felt very strongly about him. He assured us numerous times that he would take care of me and he did.

Why do good people with wonderful deeds leave Pearsall? We, the patients of Pearsall, have lost a great surgeon. It will be hard to replace a kind and generous man like him. There are many good doctors, but few add up to Dr. Carlos Soriano.

May God continue to give him strength and courage to allow him to offer the same respect to the patient of Eagle Pass. Dr. Soriano will be greatly missed by many.

The Segovia family appreciates all that he did in his short stay in Pearsall.

May God bless him richly, Dr. Soriano is my doctor, near and far.

With much appreciation,

Eutalia Segovia-Pearsall.

On August 30, 2001 another letter was sent to the *Frio-Nueces Current News*. The letter is presented verbatim below.

Dear Editor,

We would like to express our deep gratitude to Dr. Carlos Soriano for the work he did for our mother and grandmother and say how sad we will be to see him leave Pearsall.

Beatrice Barajas had never been given much hope in her medical condition until she saw Dr. Soriano and he gave her new expectations for a better life. After undergoing surgery she is in excellent health and it is because of that wonderful doctor. Where she used to need to many pills each day she now only needs two.

It's too bad that Dr. Soriano is leaving, he

would have been a great friend and doctor to so many in the community. Our family developed a close relationship with him and we hate to see him go. We wish he could stay to help others here.

Sincerely,

Gilbert Pinky Barajas and Family

Mr. & Mrs. Hoppy Chapa and Family

When I had called the agency that handled the ER schedule, they had told me that they were looking for somebody in Eagle Pass, which was a border town. I made a few phone calls and ended up talking to Dr. Sebastian Pardon, the chief of the ER in Fort Duncan Medical Center in Eagle Pass. I sent him my application and curriculum vitae (resume), and he dropped by the hospital for my interview. He found out that I was a surgeon, and Fort Duncan Medical Center was looking for a surgeon. He contacted the hospital administrator and informed him about me. I drove to Eagle Pass and met with the assistant administrator of the hospital. He showed me the hospital and the surrounding area. There was an Indian Casino, a Wal-Mart, and a small shopping mall—but no movie theaters. I was told that they are building a new hospital on the east side of Eagle Pass. He showed me a vacant office where I could build an office and said that they would guarantee my income for the first year.

I went back and forth between Pearsall and Eagle Pass several times trying to fix the office. There were two surgeons in town; we were each on call a week at a time, so the call rotation would be every three weeks. Before moving to Eagle Pass I had to go home to Florida.

In addition, my son Charles had just finished his MBA degree at Harvard in just one and a half years. The family attended his graduation ceremonies in Massachusetts.

Eagle Pass

My time in Eagle Pass, a small town of thirty-five thousand, was the last leg of my surgical practice. On December 2, 2001, I opened the office with a ribbon-cutting ceremony, which was announced in the *Eagle Pass Sunday News*. They published where I had come from as well as details on my training and experience in surgery. There were a lot of Filipinos in Eagle Pass. There was a pediatrician, as well as nurses and teachers imported from the Philippines to teach in public schools. We had Filipino gatherings most of the time to celebrate things like birthdays and other occasions just to enjoy the camaraderie.

The town had a state-sponsored outpatient clinic, including an obstetrics department; there was even a dialysis clinic, which indicates just how many diabetics with kidney complications lived in the town. I befriended an nephrologist from San Antonio who came to two days a week. He was from Pakistan and was trained in Buffalo, New York.

On my week off, I went either to San Antonio or to Del Rio, which was about an hour's drive west of Eagle Pass. They had a Regal movie theater, a bigger mall, and a Chinese restaurant.

Despite my years of practice I still continued to improve my skills. I went to Memphis to take a course on ERCP (endoscopic retrograde cholangio-pancreatogram). I had taken the same course way back in 1979 at Lahey Clinic in Boston, but during those days the technique was still in its infancy. A lot of changes had occurred since then. The procedure entails the insertion of a duodenoscope into the duodenum, the beginning of the small bowel, under fluroscopic X-ray control. Once the ampulla (opening of the bile ducts to the duodenum) was identified, a catheter was inserted, and a radiopaque dye was injected to visualize the main bile ducts and its branches. A small stone left behind during a laproscopic cholecystectomy could be removed through this procedure. I did several cases in Eagle Pass (ERCP), but that was the first time it was done in that hospital.

I kept continuing my education despite the fact that I was getting close to my retirement years. I went to Phoenix, Arizona, to learn endovascular surgery, the new way of treating peripheral vascular surgery instead of opening up the patient. This procedure is a lot less invasive. The procedure entails the insertion of a catheter into an artery in the groin area; the surgeon either goes up toward the great vessels and the heart or down toward the lower extremity and visualizes the vessels by injecting a radiopaque dye. If the vessel is narrow due to arteriosclerosis it can be expanded and dilated with the insertion of a device called a stent to maintain the patency of the vessel after dilatation. I learned this with pigs as the experimental animal and kept practicing the procedure until I got the hang of it. I did not get to do this procedure at Fort Duncan Medical Center because the administrator sold the X-ray machine. I learned a new technique that not all surgeons had the privilege of learning. This endovascular catheterization of the major vessel is part and parcel of cardiac catheterization to determine the condition of the coronary vessel of the heart, mainly performed by invasive cardiologists.

In my weeks off, I worked in the ER in Carrizo Spring about an hour's drive east of Eagle Pass. I used to work there when I was in Pearsall. The ER recruiter kept calling me. I could not say no because they were the ones who had sent me to Texas. I had to oblige them as a gesture of goodwill on my part. In that small town there was a dialysis clinic. The nurse called me up and told me that she had a patient with a clogged arteriovenous shunt. Before dialysis is started, the surgeon has to make an arterial and venous fistula for catheter insertion for dialysis. The vein in the leg is used to hook the artery up to the vein, or the surgeon can use a Dacron graft. They usually sent patients to San Antonio for that and for declogging of the fistulas. I had surgical privileges in that hospital, and in this case, I was able to improvise a catheter to remove the clot in the X-ray room of the hospital. But the following day, it clogged up again. They sent the patient to San Antonio.

Occasionally I got a consult in that hospital to do gall bladder surgery and appendectomy. The OR was barely equipped to do anything.

The Pakistani nephrologist I mentioned and I were together when he was in Eagle Pass. He was a bright physician and always gave lectures to the medical community. He lived in San Antonio with his four children and parents. After training the nephrologist group hired him in San Antonio. On my weekend trips to San Antonio we had dinner and hung out. He revealed to me that he had been in school all the time and had never had a chance to see a strip club. I said one day to him, "Okay, buddy, I will take you to one." I warned him that strip clubs were money-making businesses and that he had to be careful with his tips to the girls. It was just for visual gratification, and he was not to touch any of girls. Once you did that you would have to deal with the bouncer of the club. I took him to one club where the women were totally exposed. He enjoyed it visually, but that's about it.

Life went on in Eagle Pass without much hassle. The doctor on call in the emergency room was also obliged to be on call on the floor for consultations. I did a lot of laparoscopic cholecystectomies and laparoscopic appendectomies in children. In one case I had a consultation from a pediatrician. The child complained of low abdominal pain. I have seen the patient for several days in a row and was monitoring her abdomen. I could not convince myself that the child had appendicitis. My examination was based purely on physical examination because the white count (white blood cells) is not reliable on kids. Every time a child gets sick for whatever reason, the white count usually goes up. Even a simple cold will do that. I told the pediatrician that I didn't think it was appendicitis. He got a second opinion from a gung-ho surgeon. He operated on the kid, and the nurse showed me the specimen when I was doing a colonoscopy. The appendix was red all right, but there was no sign of exudate on its wall, meaning it was not inflamed at all. I heard that the kid developed a complication and was transferred to San Antonio. The case was presented in the surgical conference, and I heard that the surgeon was lectured by the receiving surgeon in San Antonio for operating on a child when he had no business in doing the appendectomy if he could not take care of the complication. Would you believe that the reason he gave was that he operated on the child because I would not operate? *What kind of reasoning is that?* I asked myself. Nobody said anything, and I totally ignored it, because I don't dwell on unreasonable premises.

The cases I got from the ER were something else. We

were right on the border of Mexico, with the Rio Grand river separating it from the United States. When you crossed the bridge you were in a different country. Most residents in Eagle Pass went there for dental work and to buy medications. The town in Mexico across the bridge was called Piedras Negras, and the residents in turn crossed the bridge into Texas to go to Wal-Mart.

There is a federal law that any patient who comes in through the ER cannot be turned down, whether he or she is a citizen or not. You have to take care of the patient no matter what. I had several patients transferred from across the border with screwed-up surgery and also major surgical injuries. Sometimes we had to transfer patients to San Antonio; they didn't like the idea but couldn't do anything about it.

My wife came for a visit one day, and I took her to Corpus Christi, the very southern part of Texas. It had been a small fishing village many years ago that became a big metropolitan area with a lot of seafood and seaside attractions. An old War II aircraft carrier, the USS *Lexington*, was moored permanently there for the tourists to enjoy.

The house I was living in was rented from one of the internists who worked in the hospital. He promised me he would send me cases to help my practice. He also had a pediatrician brother who would refer me cases. Remember Dr. Norton from Seminole who had stopped sending me patients when I refused to rent his office building? Well, I was not going to repeat the same mistake again.

My practice continued to struggle; I had difficulties due to the poor patient load and also Medicaid and non-paying patients. I had tried opening another office twice a week in Carrizo Springs for several months but barely broke even there. The town was not big enough to support a surgeon, but I still worked in their emergency room and took consults in the hospital.

I was sixty-four-years-old by then, and my vision was not getting any better—probably from cataracts. During one of my laparoscopic cholecystectomies I accidentally divided the common duct while trying to remove the gall bladder. The common or main duct varies in length and configuration. I immediately recognized the problem, so I opened the patient and repaired the injury. The patient had an uneventful postoperative course. That was my first accident since the very beginning of my practice, and I thought it was about time to quit surgery altogether. My vision was not as sharp as it used to be.

In the early months of 2004, the hospital notified me that my BNNDD permit had expired. This permit is issued by the government to allow physicians to prescribe narcotics and controlled substances. I had not received anything in the mail about it, probably because I had moved from one place to the other and the renewal notification did not get to me. The administrator requested that I file for a leave of absence while waiting for the renewal, and I received it a few weeks later.

The biggest problem in surgical practices all over the United States is malpractice insurance. I was being charged an arm and a leg. I informed the administrator about my problem and asked what he could do. He made a few phone calls to the main headquarters in Philadelphia, and I was told that they could not help me. He tried his best to convince me to stay, but I could not. In June of 2004 I packed my bags, gave my books to the hospital library, and headed home to Florida for my retirement.

THE FAMILY

GRANDCHILDREN

Epilogue

We all know that hindsight is always 20/20. Viewing my life as a whole has given me the perspective that my formative years prepared me for the life that lay ahead. My first twenty-five years on earth gave me the chance to change my life from a very humble beginning and to help me become a very successful person all on my own and with the help of somebody up there who guided my decisions about what course to take to achieve the unachievable.

The people who nurtured me with love gave me the strength and willpower to be who I am now. My childhood adventures of making things out of my bare hands along with a little common sense and imagination grew into the dexterity that allowed me to be a successful surgeon. They say that wisdom is the product of knowledge and experience, and I would add to that common sense. All the decisions I made from day one were made with the consideration of pros and cons, devoid of emotion, taking care that no decision would have any adverse effect on anyone. This is exemplified by my operating on my wife twice and delivering my first child myself.

I said before that somebody up there guided my decisions, and—even better—somebody up there liked me. Now I know the reasons for my academic failure when I was in the college of medicine and for selling my outlines (OB-GYN, of all things) to pay for my tuition and books. Everything that happens on earth has a reason. You may not know it in that particular moment, but later you find out. The decisions you make in your early life might give you a good result or an adverse effect. Kids nowadays make snap decisions in the early stages of their lives that may have great consequences. Drugs, poor living conditions, peer pressure, or whatever, there is no reason to be led astray. In the United States of America, there are grants, scholarships, and government aid programs that will help you if you are resourceful enough and persistent. Remember, tomorrow is another day!

It has been my inherent nature to organize, and I have an uncanny ability to see somewhat what lies ahead. Could it have been gut feeling or intuition? That, I don't know. I just knew what lay ahead.

Before I left the Philippines I tried to organize a community association in my neighborhood but because I was leaving for the United States it didn't pan out. Could that be the reason that I was the founder and co-founder of various organizations in Pinellas County that still exist today? Could it be that I was the recipient of the key to the City of St. Petersburg? Or could it be the culmination of my long-time dream of organizing the Filipinos with the establishment of the first building of its kind in the United States, the Philippine Cultural Center in Oldsmar? I still don't know the reasons, but whatever they are, the outcome is done deal! I will surely know in the future if I am still alive.

I fulfilled all my promises to my grandmother in helping my parents and my two sisters. I kept the promise I made to myself to send all my children to private schools and colleges without the headache and trauma I suffered when I was growing up and going through school. Maybe they will understand me upon reading my biography.

I am not a genius in the true sense of the word. I am just a driven and motivated person, whose life is ruled by honesty and integrity—and indeed, a lot of common sense.

My mind keeps working all the time, incessantly. I have to shut it off at night by taking tranquilizers just to put me to sleep and avoid a long, sleepless night. Healthwise, I am in good shape; I take care of myself medically. I still feel that I have one more lap to go before saying goodbye. I have grandchildren to take care of to continue my legacy.

Whenever I plan something in life, there is always a Plan B up my sleeve; and I always aim for the top knowing that I can always scale down if I need to. All my endeavors have been successful so far. Will things change? Only time will tell.

Guidelines for Harmony

Whoever created the world with its inhabitants made an imperfect creation. There is a man and a woman and a combination of both .

These created ambiguity and confusion since the beginning of times. The church declare it a sin and the states were in total chaos how to deal with with it up to the present time. We are all human beings and should be treated with respect and dignity. It is not for us to judge whether the creation is perfect or imperfect - they are humans.

1) Do not impose your will upon others for there will be opposition
2) Respect the opinion of others, it may or may not be line with yours.
3) Don't give somebody a guilt complex, he or she will be in a defensive mode and eventually will trigger and aggressive mode.
4) Don't talk to somebody loudly or with a strong audible

" loud talking" noise directing your comments to somebody else, talk to that particular person you may learn something new (parinig).

5) Stop playing the "Blaming Game" that is, "it's his fault" or somebody else fault. We are not perfect, we make mistakes instead of blaming somebody try to solve the problem. It is very demoralizing to the person you are blaming. For sure harmony will be disrupted.

6) Don't hold a grudge or hateful feelings in your heart against somebody, for they will slowly erode your inner shelf.

7) Don't be a negative person, be optimistic and a positive thinker for that will be good for your inner self. It is the belief that good ultimately predominates over evil.

8) Don't gossip, if you have to please tell only the truth and nothing else

9) Remember the 10 Commandments "Thou shall not bear false witness against they neighbor".

10) If you are blessed with great wealth and or higher education, be humble, not all people are blessed like you.

11) For those of you with a superiority complex for whatever reasons be it your race and or wealth be humble, you are not different from anybody.

12) If you think you are better for whatever reason, there is always somebody out there better than you.

13) If wisdom is defined as a combination of knowledge and experience - would add to that - common sense.

14) Remember what your grandmother have told you? "If you cannot say something nice, keep your mouth shut".

15) Remember what confucius said: "what you do not wish done to yourself, do not do to others"

16) He also said: "feel kindly to everyone, but be intimate only with the virtuous"

17) We worship only one god but in various different ways be it Judaism, Catholism,Hinduism, Buddahism, Islam and some other minor religion.

18) Remember the Beatitudes of Jesus:

"Blessed are the merciful for they shall obtain mercy".

"Blessed are the pure of heart for they shall see God".

"Blessed are the peacemaker for they shall be called the children of God".

Bibliography

Baucum Phd.D, Don "Pyschology Second Edition" (Barron's EZ-101 Study Keys). Barron's Educational Series, Inc. Hauppauge, New York, 1999.

Editor's Notes, Frio-Nueces Current News " Hard to Replace, August 16 and 30th 2001 Pearsall, Texas.

The Philippine Cultural Foundation, Inc. "Bayanihan Arts Center" Who's Who, First Edition, 2003.

Steinberg, Rafael "Return to the Phlippines" Time-Life Books Chicago, Illinois - 1980.

Smith,Huston, "The World's Religions" Revised and Updated Edition 1986, Harper-Collins Publishers, 10 East 53rd Street, New York, N.Y. 10022.

Zaide, Gregorio F. & Zaide, Sonia M. Phlippine History & Government". National Book Store, Inc. Metro-Manila-1987.

Special appreciation for the literary contributions of:
Claire Ick
Robert Ruelo, Esq.
Inicita Soriano Maslog